REFLECTIONS ON ART, LIFE, AND ITALY

REFLECTIONS ON ART, LIFE, AND ITALY

sunset valley press

BY SUPRIYA KHAROD

The events and conversations in this book have been set down to the best of the author's ability and memory and have been represented as faithfully as possible. The information in this book was correct at the time of publication, but the Author does not assume any liability for loss or damage caused by errors or omissions.

ISBN 978-1-7363126-0-5

Library of Congress Control Number 2020924842

Published by Sunset Valley Press
www.sunsetvalleypress.com
www.supriyakharod.com

In 2002, my husband Ketan and I spent six days in Italy as part of a longer European adventure. The anecdotes featured here occurred during that brief time period. The art, writing, and reflection manifested over the next 18 years. Although many of the reflections are on my art process, each holds a larger life lesson as well; because through art, I understand life. I hope you smile at the anecdotes, discover how an artist's mind works, and contemplate on the reflections.

This book is dedicated to my father who was an avid traveler and student of world cultures. He always told me, "You can't truly see a country until you get lost in it."

ROME

"Palatine Sky" - 11 x 15 watercolor

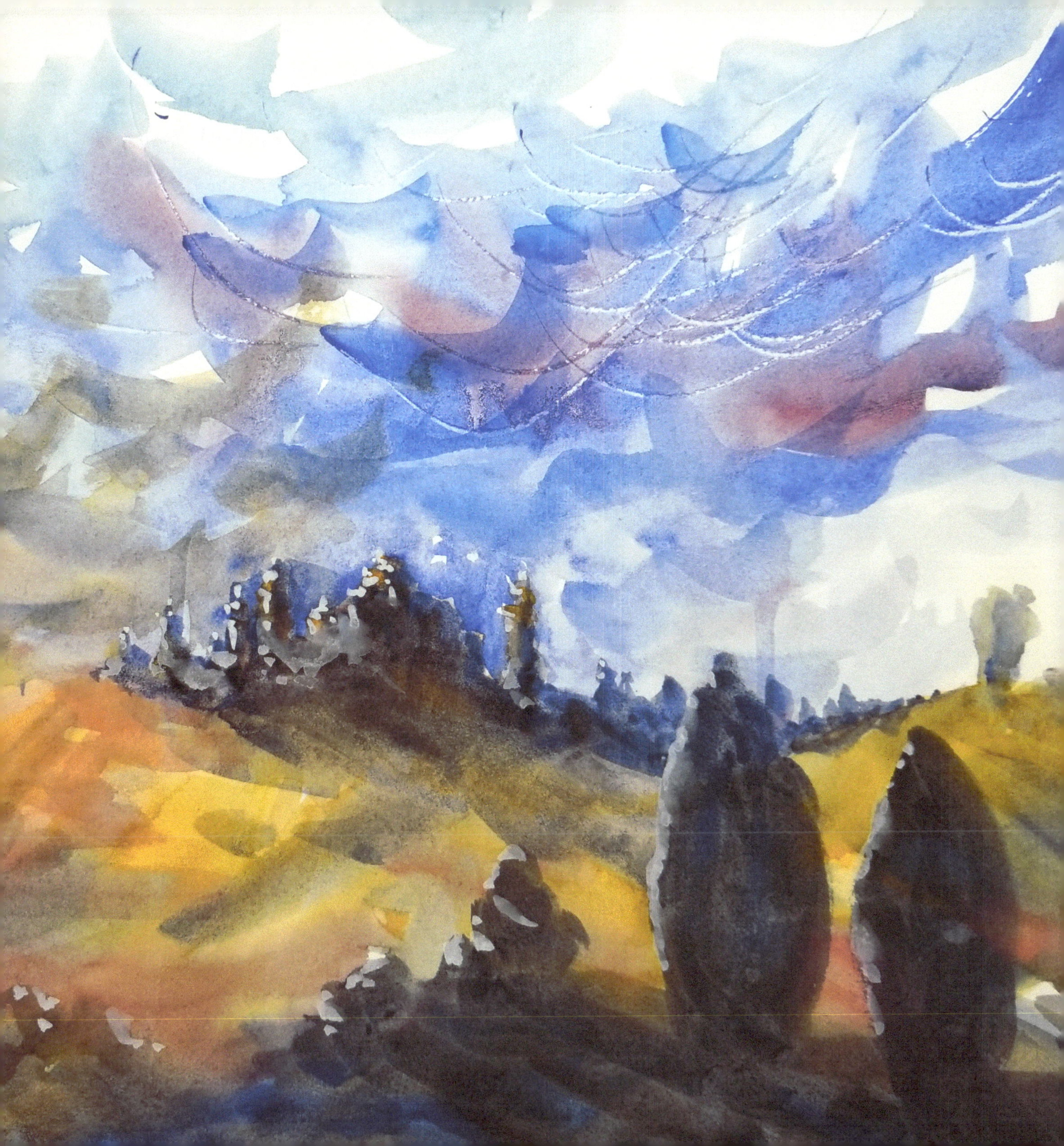

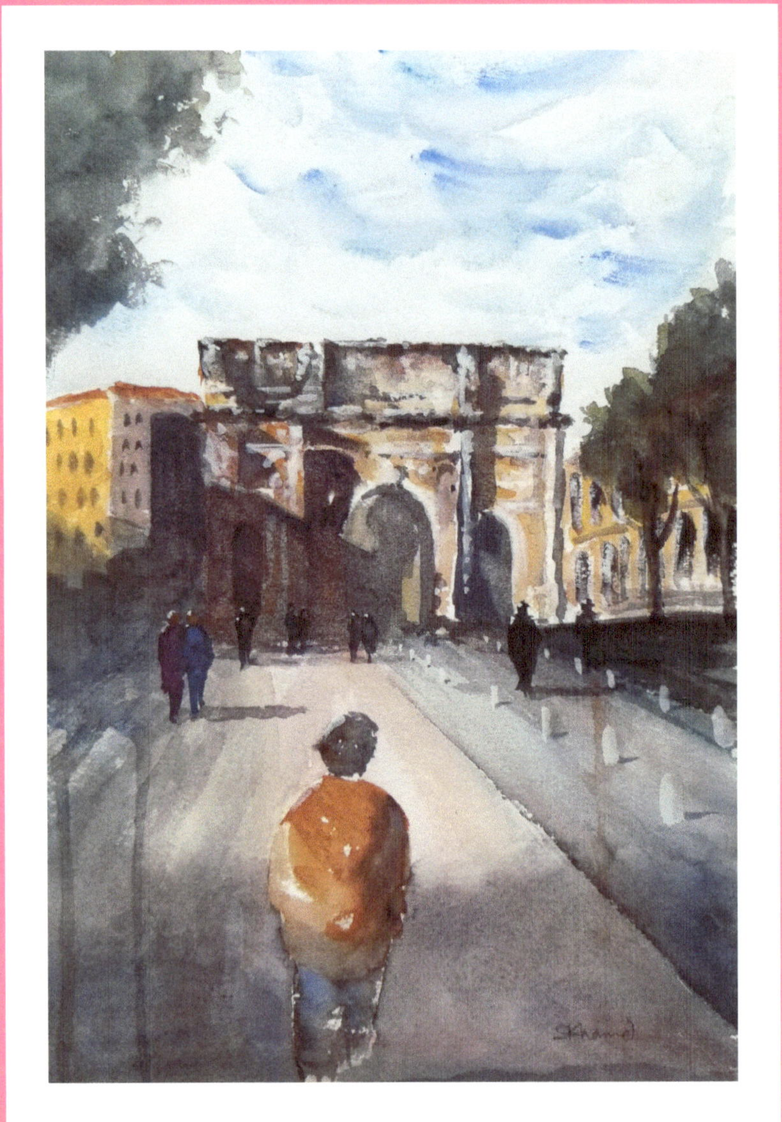

"The trees look like broccoli and every other building is a ruin!" were my first impressions of the Eternal City.

My American eye was getting pulled simultaneously in all directions. The ubiquitous 'broccoli' trees and stone buildings were mere backdrops for zigzagging vehicles and busy pedestrians. People around us were conversing animatedly in rapid-fire Italian. Above us, planters stuffed with colorful flowers and clothes drying on sagging clotheslines cohabitated apartment building balconies. And the gates leading into these apartment buildings looked like entrances to museums.

I noticed a gentleman, wearing a light peach suit and colorful shoes, rushing to work. And nearby, both locals and tourists were staring at a lady (who was accessorized to the hilt) sporting bright red pants.

Wonderstruck by all these enthralling sights of Rome, I realized I should perhaps close my dropped jaw and instead, look at the world-famous monuments before me.

"Arch of Constantine" - 10 x 14 watercolor

"How 'bout them Longhorns?"

When two Americans meet while traveling abroad, they tend to gravitate towards one another. When two Austinites meet while traveling abroad, they gravitate towards one another and talk about the Texas Longhorns. The following encounter was our introduction to this fundamental truth.

One evening, my husband Ketan and I were about to embark on a group tour of the Imperial Forum. As we were waiting, another couple approached us and introduced themselves. This is the conversation that ensued:

Them: "Hello! We noticed your UT shirt. We're from Austin too."

Us: "Cool. Nice to meet you, 5000 miles away from home."

Them: "So, do you know what was the score of the game today?"

Alas, we didn't. But we enjoyed our tour of the Forum with our new acquaintances and cheerfully discussed how this was definitely the year the Longhorns would go all the way (they didn't).

During the remainder of our Italian campaign, we did not meet any other Austinites, unfortunately.

"Imperial Forum" - 8 x 10 pencil, artist's collection

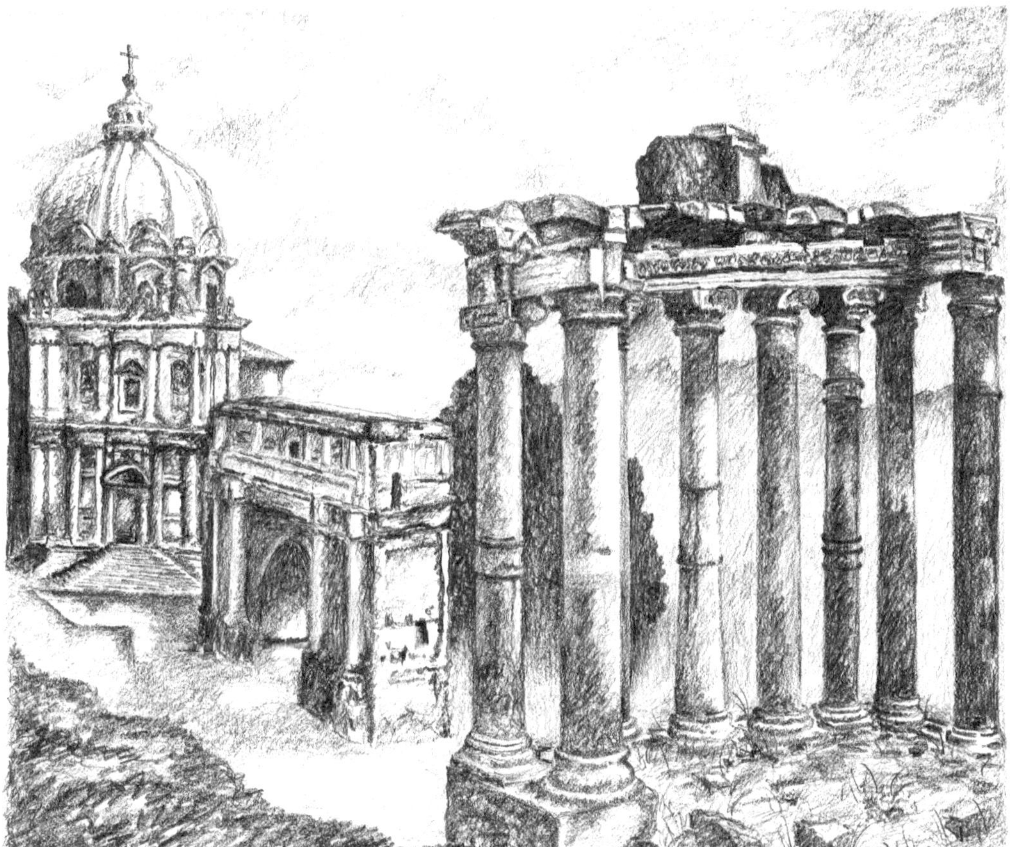

IMPERIAL FORUM, ROME

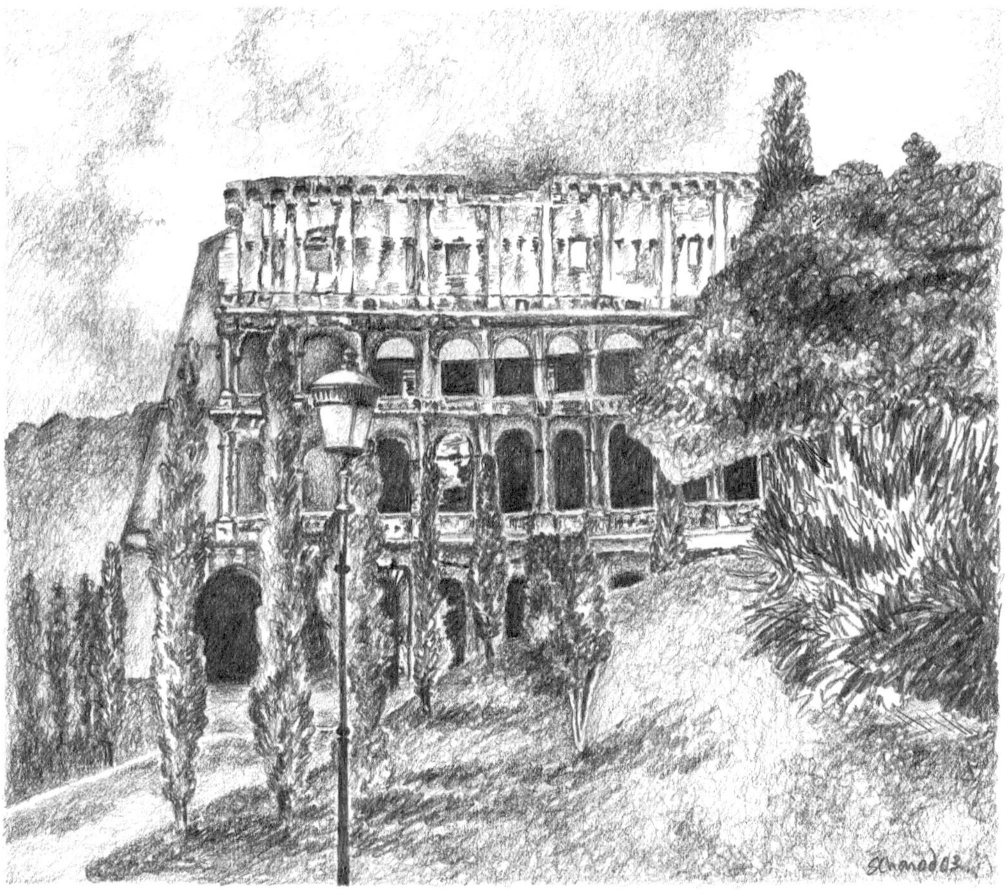

COLOSSEUM, ROME

Looking back on that experience, I asked myself, had we met those same people back in Austin, would we have even noticed them? Probably not. But thousands of miles away, in a foreign land, we immediately connected with them over something familiar—UT football.

The universe brings people into our lives for a reason. Sometimes, that reason is just to kindle a flash of unexpected joy in our hearts.

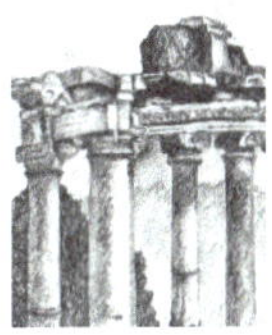

When we humans discover a commonality with one another, it creates a 'tiny spark' of connection between us. The experience at the Forum made me think about how these 'tiny sparks' occur. The universe brings people together, but *we* must make an effort to make the connection. Some simple methods are to make eye contact, smile, and say hello. If that Austin couple hadn't initiated conversation, we would have missed having this delightful interaction. So, treat every opportunity life provides as a gift from the universe to create a 'tiny spark.'

"Colosseum" - 8 x 10 pencil, artist's collection

Shorts not allowed

The next day, we discovered the Pantheon while walking about. I entered the ancient Roman temple alone, as Ketan was wearing shorts and was not permitted inside. (Toga-wearing gods should be more forgiving, I think).

Inside the spectacular temple, a single beam of light fell from a small, circular opening in the dome—the oculus—onto the magnificent marble floor below. As in most ancient Roman temples, the art and architecture were absolutely awe-inspiring. So, I felt a twinge of sadness that Ketan could not experience it firsthand with me.

Standing inside the Pantheon made me fondly recall an incident from my early days in advertising. Once, my copywriter partner and I (the art director) had come up with (what we felt) a fantastic idea to shoot a television commercial inside the Pantheon—complete with a dove flying out of a sunlit oculus at the end. Our suspicious creative director saw through it and commented, "It sounds like you two are trying hard to find a way to visit Rome, aren't you?" My partner and I both tried to look extremely innocent, but, alas, to no avail. A commercial shoot in Rome was just not in our stars.

"Pantheon" - 8 x 10 pencil, artist's collection

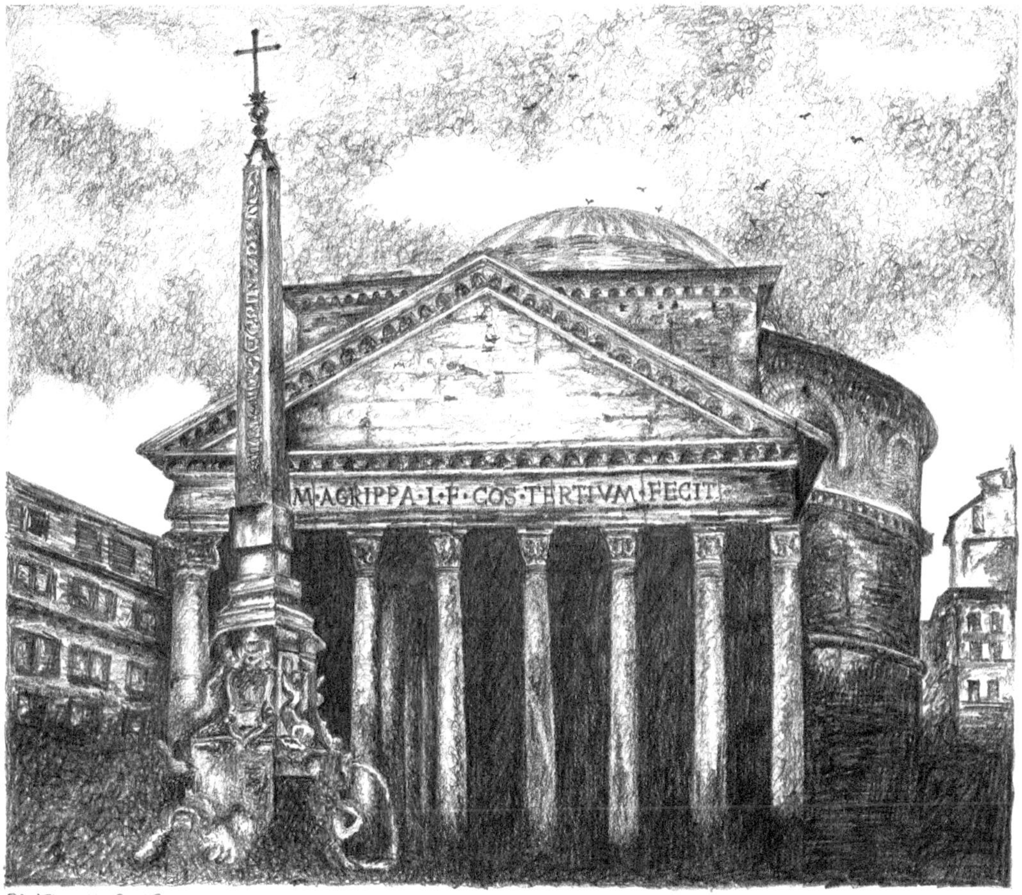

PANTHEON, ROME

SURE! WHY NOT?

When it comes to art, my mantra is, "Sure! Why not?" and I try to push traditional norms. So, for the pencil sketches in this book, I challenged myself to draw all the monuments without using a ruler. Could I? Sure! Why not?

Then, the next question was, "How do I draw a long, straight line?"

First, I decided to focus on one small segment of the long line and concentrate on making it straight. Then, I drew more small segments, focusing on one at a time, until they came together to form a long, straight line. Was I able to draw a straight line because I believed I could? Or did my small-segment strategy actually work?

Whichever it was, I realized two important lessons:

1. My mind has great power to create and influence my reality.

2. To make the end result amazing, I must exert my best effort and put full focus into making each tiny step excellent.

When each of those tiny steps is excellent, the end result becomes supremely satisfying and can even elicit a "Wow, I didn't realize I could do that!" reaction.

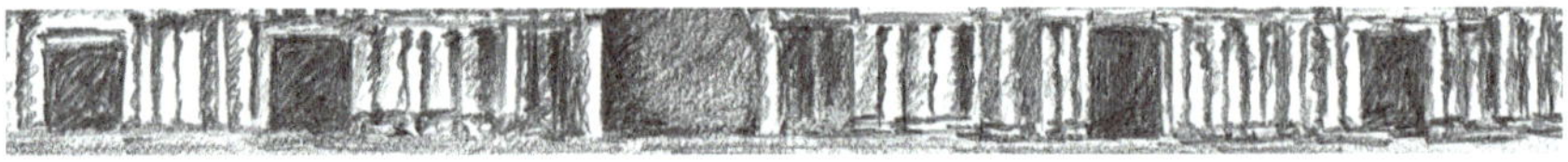

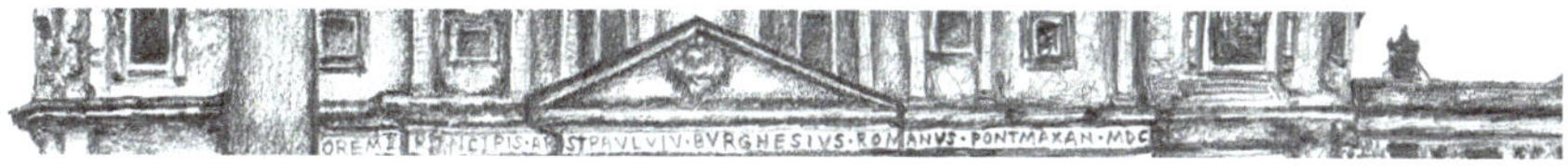

As a second drawing challenge, I chose to sketch using only a simple mechanical pencil and no blending tools. Traditionally, a blending tool is used to smudge pencil strokes and to create soft, shaded transitions. But in my sketches, all the drawing and shading would be accomplished with only pure line work.

After drawing a light initial sketch to plan the composition, I began shading. By placing tiny strokes in a loose formation with a light touch, I created light grays. To achieve darker grays and blacks, I placed strokes more tightly together while applying firm pressure on the pencil. By shading in this way, I capitalized on the mechanical pencil's strength—the ability to create fine, precise lines.

What is your strength? Are you an artist? A compassionate friend? An optimist? An attentive listener? Find one strength you have and focus on expanding it. In movies, the superhero always stands tall, with head up and chest expanded. He is confident because he knows what his strength is and his confidence radiates out to the world. So, have a confident superhero attitude by expanding your strength. The same way a humble mechanical pencil can create a beautiful drawing, your strength can define you in the world's eyes.

SUPERHERO ATTITUDE

VENICE

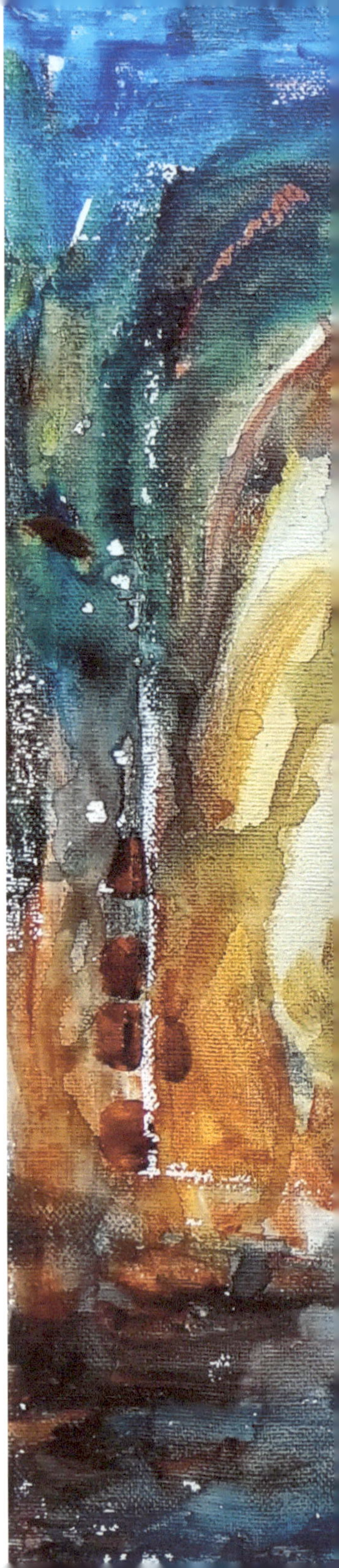

“Sunset Over Venice” - 16 x 20 watercolor on canvas, private collection

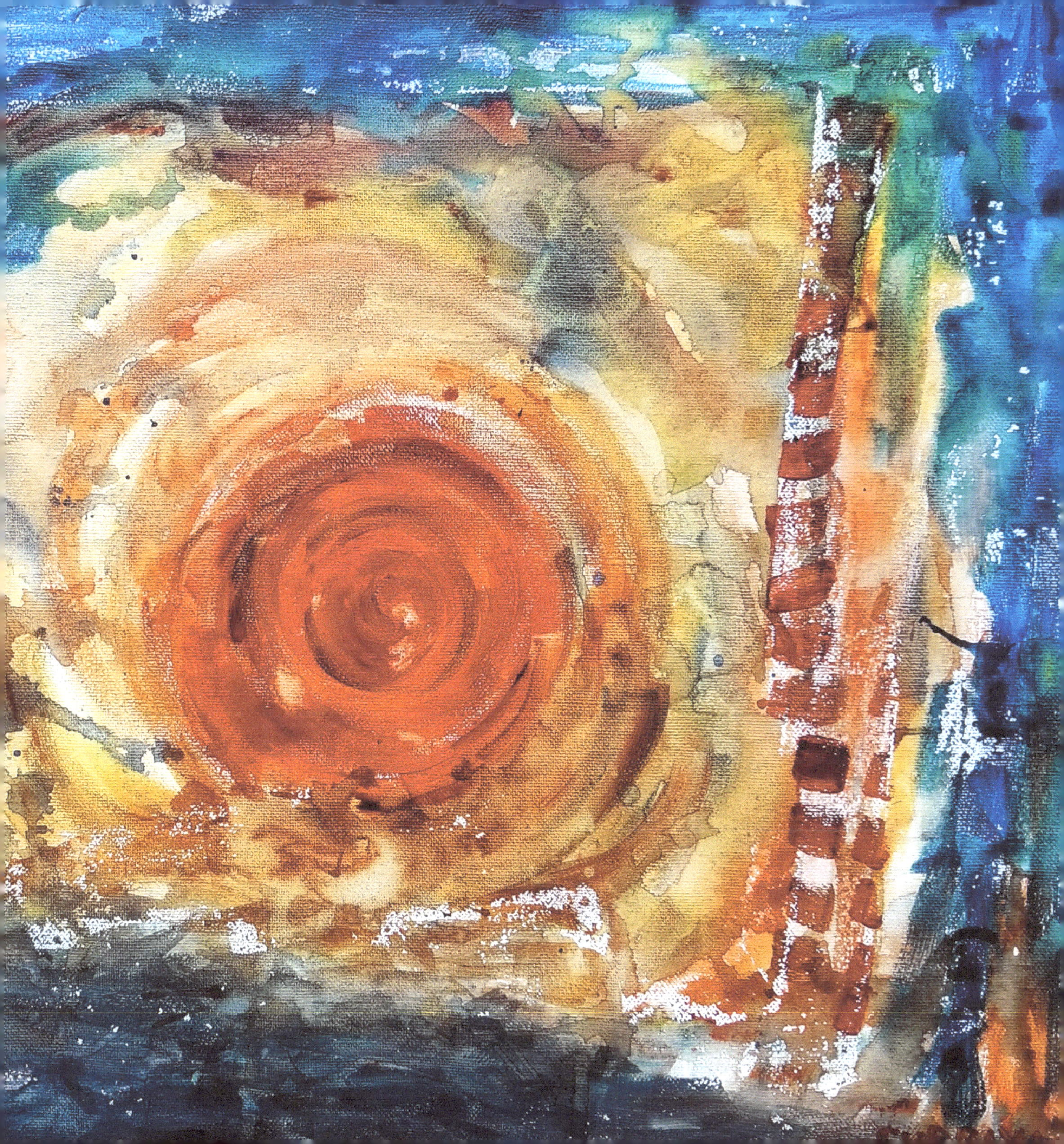

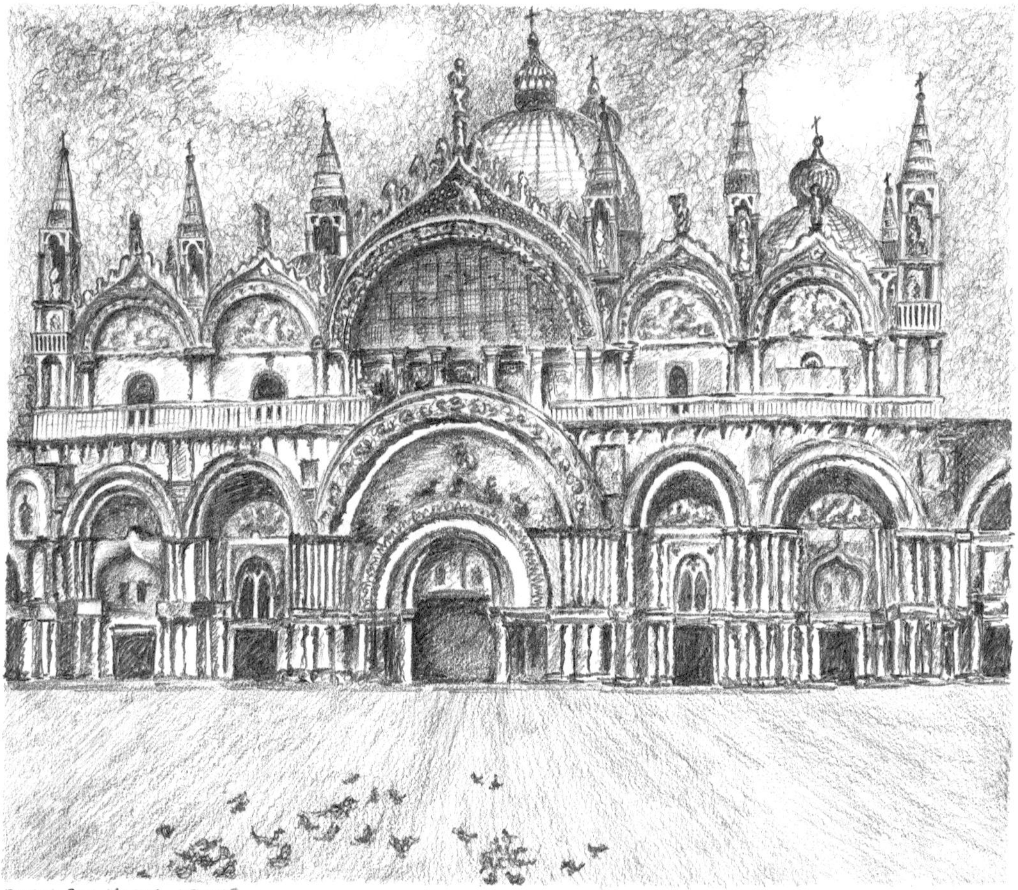

PIAZZA SAN MARCO, VENICE

Clean hair. Narrow alleyways. Waiting pigeons. Not good.

They seemed so innocent—sitting in St. Mark's Plaza, pecking at the birdseed fed by overzealous tourists. But somehow they knew. And I knew they knew. And then, on our last day in Venice, it happened. Hundreds of pigeons, perched on the eaves in narrow alleys by the shops, were waiting for that ripe moment for me to pass underneath. And they were rewarded.

We rushed back to the hotel (so I could wash my hair) and then ran to catch our train (which we caught by the skin of our teeth). I'm sure other tourists can sympathize with my plight. Walking around the alleys in Venice made me feel like Tippi Hedren in Alfred Hitchcock's "The Birds." The key difference is that pigeon poop is less life-threatening than beaks and wings, fortunately.

"Piazza San Marco" - 8 x 10 pencil, artist's collection

Life before GPS

As if watching our heads were not enough, we had to watch the roads too. Crooked streets and narrow alleys crisscrossed randomly. Signs led everywhere. And nowhere. Just as we thought we had found our route, a canal forced us to take a circuitous detour. We got lost. And lost. And lost. (This is what life before GPS looked like.)

Ketan, who has out-of-this-world navigational skills and can read maps as easily as he can read Dr. Seuss books, was also beaten by the maps of Venice. But, in all fairness, I don't think Venetian maps are drawn very well. They look more like medical textbook renderings of the body's vascular system, where every teeny tiny artery and vein is pictured. But, on a map, when teeny tiny lines branch off of main roads everywhere (yet don't seem to exist in real life), you can have a major problem.

Fortunately, watching the beautiful canals, gondolas, monuments, people, food, and never-ending shops overshadowed the experiences of continually losing our way and getting "pigeoned on."

"Pigeon Alley" - 10 x 14 watercolor

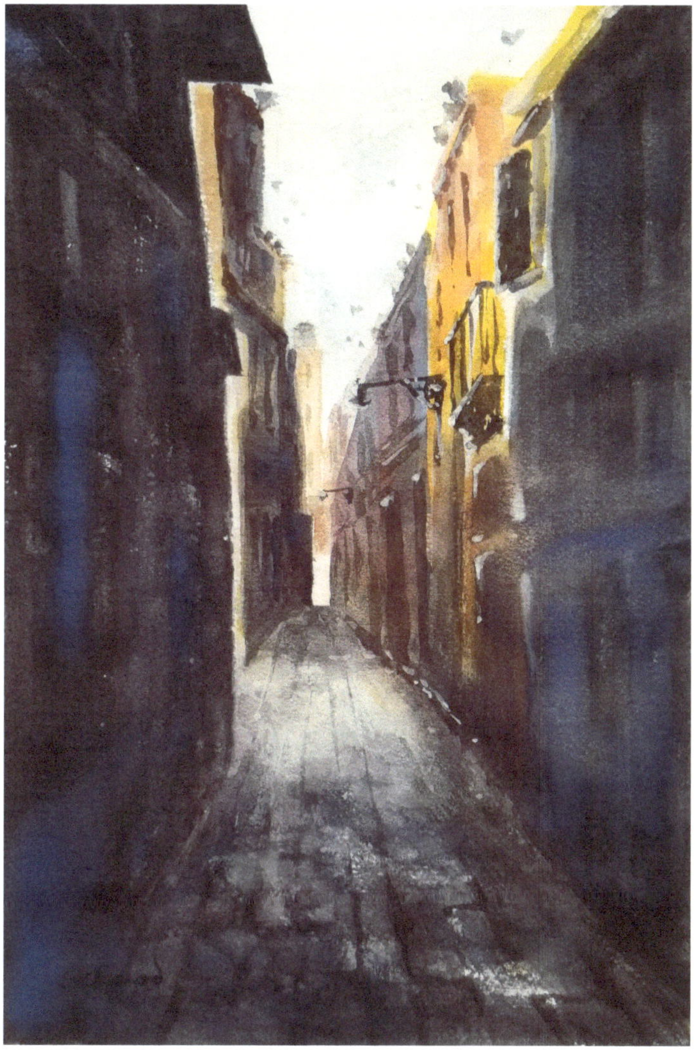

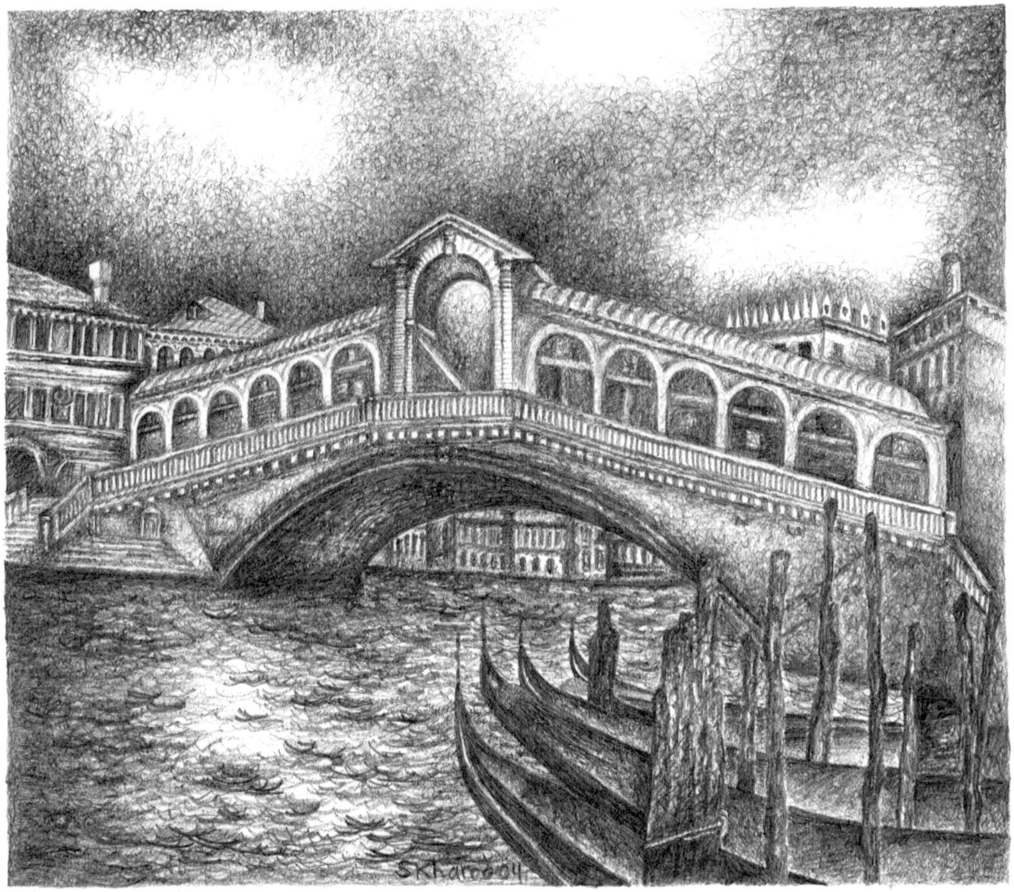

RIALTO BRIDGE, VENICE

A gelato a day keeps the walking-miles-over-tiny-bridges-and-cobblestones-while-getting-lost soreness away

Gelato, Italian ice cream, is phenomenal. One day, Ketan decided to buy gelatos. I said (foolishly), "That's cool. You get one. I'll taste a bit out of it. But I don't need an entire one for myself right now." So, he bought himself a chocolate gelato and we continued on our way.

A little later, feeling sympathetic, he offered me some of his. So, I had a lick. One lick turned into two. Two, into four. That turned into, "Um, can I get it back?" Returning to the gelato cart to buy another one was not an option because there was no guarantee we would actually find it again (reference "Life before GPS").

I don't know if I learned the bigger lesson that day or my husband did.

My takeaway: A missed opportunity may not present itself again and trying to find your way back can be your bane. Life is full of opportunities. Do you seize them or do you spend the rest of your life wondering wistfully, "If only I had...?" You can never fully live in the present if you spend all your time looking back. And repeatedly taking advantage of your husband's generous nature, in this way, is not cool.

His takeaway: Always get two gelatos.

"Rialto Bridge" - 8 x 10 pencil, artist's collection

I am inspired by J.M.W. Turner, a British painter, and John Singer Sargent, an American painter. Both are considered definitive masters of watercolor. Turner's watercolors are beautifully minimal and demonstrate dynamic color harmony, brushwork, and atmospheric drama. Sargent's watercolors exquisitely capture the light, display precise brushwork, and showcase bold colors. By studying the work of such masters, I learn how to apply the fundamentals to my own paintings and, through this process of learning, discover my own style.

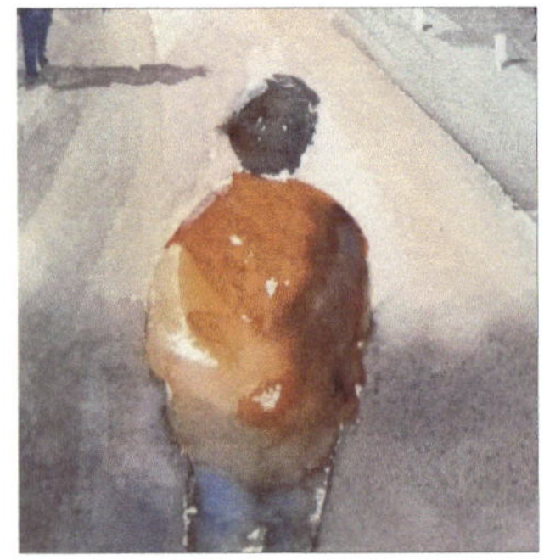

Be honest. If you keep telling yourself what you want to hear, you'll never tell yourself what you need to hear.

Study and self-reflection are essential for all artists. When I look at a completed painting, I ask myself: Did I capture the atmosphere and mood I had envisioned in my head? Did I show just enough of the subject without spelling out every detail? Did my color choices harmonize well? Were my brushstrokes confident? Did I tell a story? It can be difficult to answer 'no' to any of these questions. But an honest answer—which may be an unpleasant, yet necessary, truth—is the first step towards an artist's growth.

We often reflect on, "What went wrong?" How often do we reflect on, "What went right?"

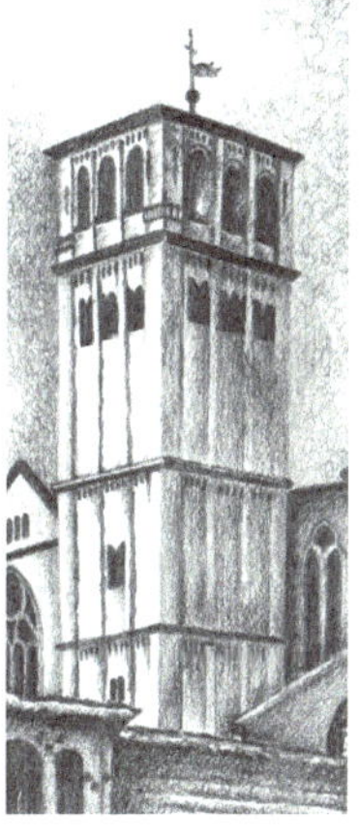

When a completed painting doesn't look very good (this happens from time to time), the artist quickly begins to reflect upon what went wrong. When a painting turns out beautifully though, the same artist will set it aside without much further thought and move to the next one.

I have learned not to do that. After asking, "What went wrong?" I also ask myself, "What went right?" Asking this second question accomplishes two things. First, it helps me realize that even in the most unsuccessful painting, at least one element worked well. That element may not even be related to art. It could be, for example, that I went out of my comfort zone and tried something new. Second, when I understand both 'what went wrong' and 'what went right,' I can correct the wrong or replicate the right in my next effort.

You learn and grow by questioning the 'wrongs' and you gain self-confidence by examining the 'rights.' Whether in art or life, practice looking at not only 'what went wrong,' but also at 'what went right' and see where your reflections lead you.

Why is it romantic to glide in a gondola under a bridge that led prisoners to their deaths?

This is one of the mysteries of the Bridge of Sighs I will never understand. A popular theory is that if a couple kisses under the Bridge while gliding in a gondola, they will enjoy eternal love. My theory is that this theory was postulated and circulated by gondoliers (boatmen who drive the gondolas) to drum up support for their enterprise. But, it is a beautiful bridge nonetheless.

We chose to take a tour of the Doge's Palace, which culminated by walking through the Bridge of Sighs to the dungeons. Historically, the Bridge was the last chance a prisoner saw the world (and sighed) as he was ushered to either long-term imprisonment or to death in the dungeons.

As we crossed the Bridge, I stuck my hand out of a small window and waved exuberantly. As I did so, I heard an excited buzz from the tourists outside— "Look, it's a hand!" I wonder why they were shocked to see a hand waving out of the window? They couldn't have thought it was a modern-day prisoner, could they?

"Bridge of Sighs" - 8 x 10 pencil, artist's collection

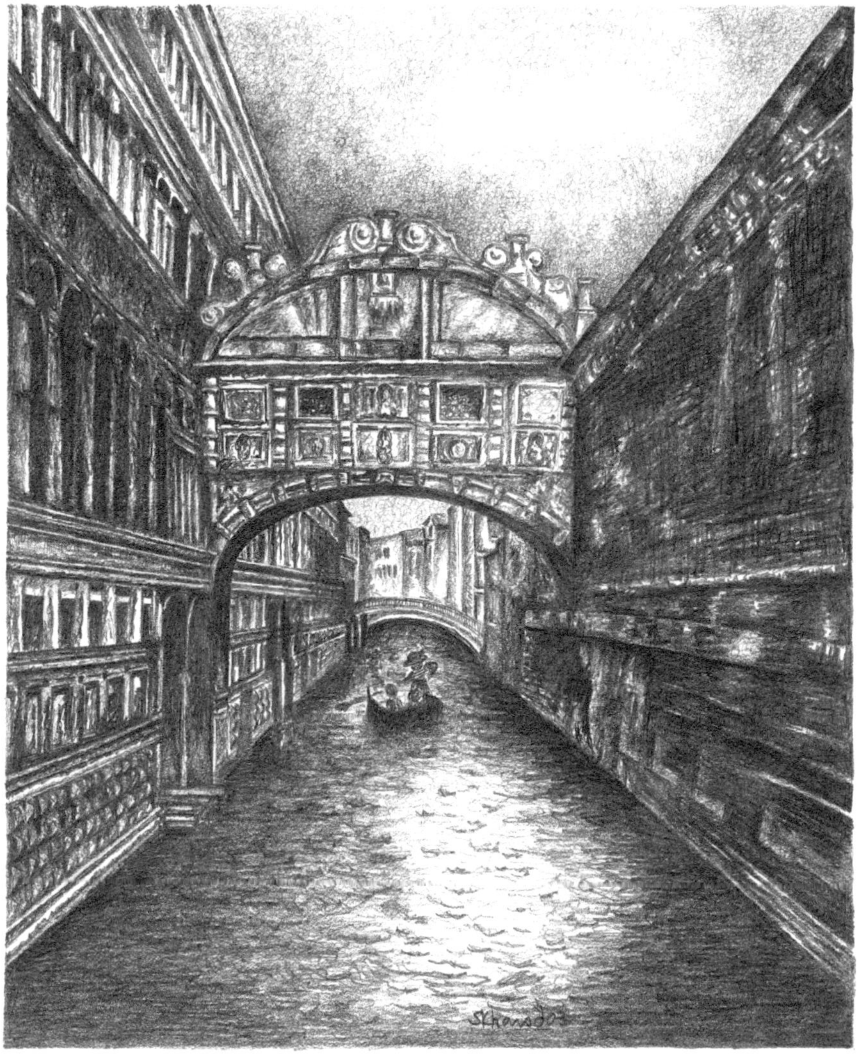

BRIDGE OF SIGHS, VENICE

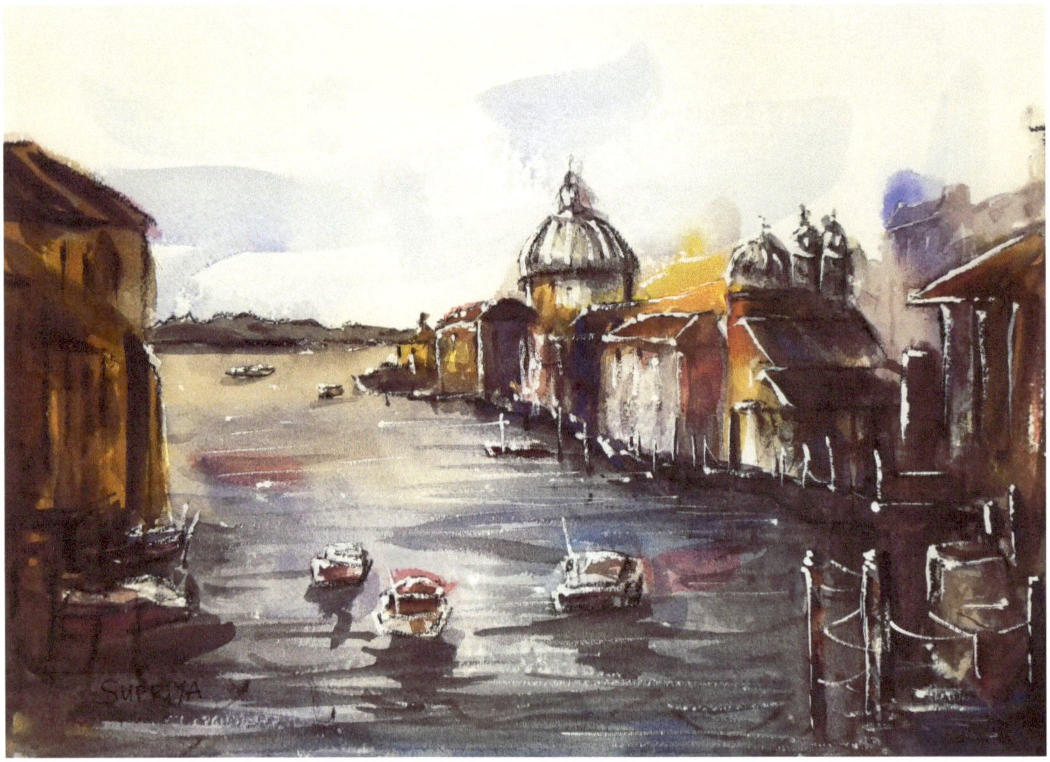
SUPRIYA

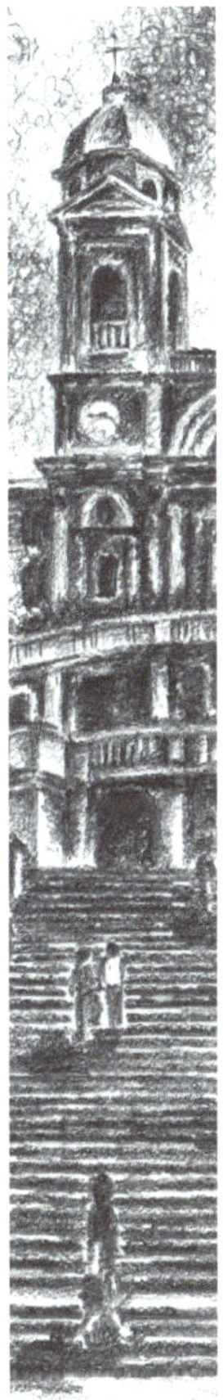

In addition to being inspired by Turner and Sargent, I am influenced by Claude Monet, the French Impressionist painter. Monet masterfully created both large and small-scale paintings using carefully-placed, colorful dabs of paint on his canvases. When you view his paintings up close, you can see thousands of small brushstrokes, which appear almost haphazard. But, when seen from across the room, waterlilies, sunsets, fields, and people emerge almost magically and make you realize that each stroke was actually painted quite thoughtfully. In this way, Impressionists tricked the eye by positioning colors and shapes together strategically to create an 'impression' of an image in the viewer's brain.

When I paint crowds, rooftops, and scenes depicting general 'busyness,' I strive to emulate Monet's optical trickery by using small strokes of color. If you view a painting from near, colors and brushstrokes appear to be placed randomly. But, if you look from further away, you may start seeing sense in what you had previously perceived as nonsense.

Sometimes you have to step back to see what is right in front of your eyes.

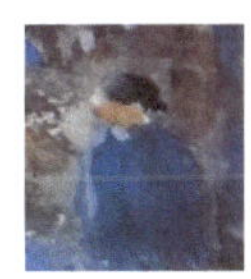

Try it with the paintings in this book. Do you see a different perspective by standing further away? Now, look at difficult situations in life. Do you see a different perspective by standing further away?

"The Grand Canal #1" - 10 x 13 watercolor, private collection

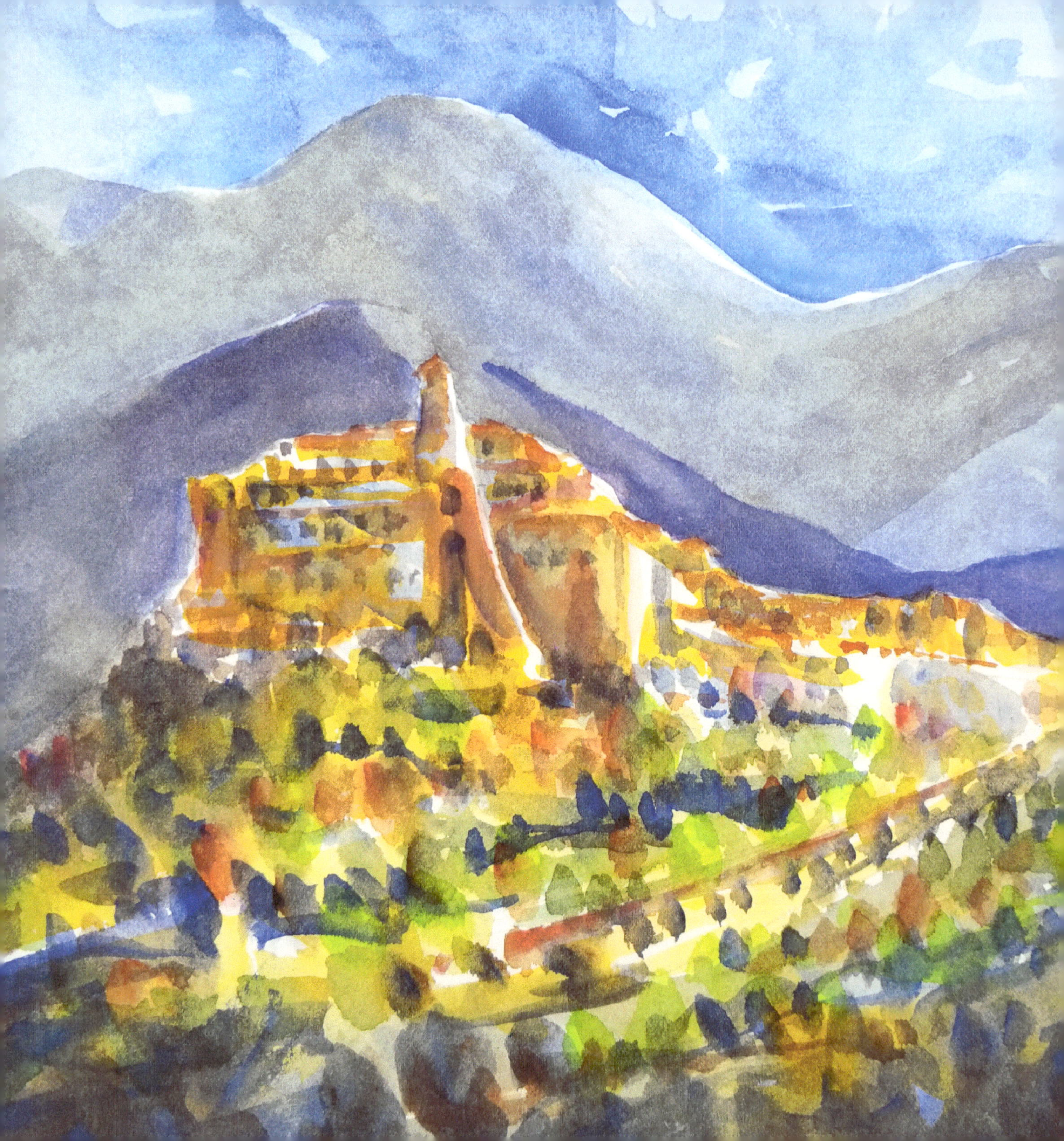

ASSISI

"The Fortress City" - 11 x 15 watercolor

I was ten years old when my spiritual education teacher asked our class to memorize the *Prayer of St. Francis,* "O Lord, make me an instrument of thy peace..." Even after growing older, St. Francis's words on peace always remained in my mind and heart.

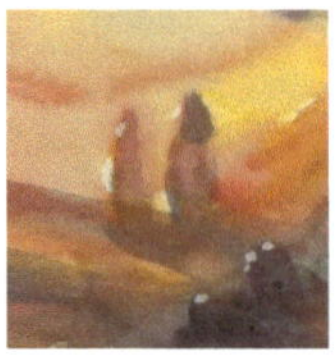

The line that resonates with me the most is, "O Divine Master, grant that I may not so much seek... to be understood, as to understand."

How do we understand? Understanding is not the same as comprehension. It comes from listening to others with open ears, closed mouth, and a non-judgmental mind.

Listening, in this way, cultivates an understanding of others and the world. That understanding then promotes self-reflection, growth, and, ultimately, inner peace. Then only, you become an instrument of peace in the world.

In Italy, when language was a barrier, we could have become impatient and frustrated. Instead, we chose to listen, smile, and use gestures to communicate. It may sound overly simplistic, but the first step to understanding is listening. Because, as the saying goes, "God gave us two ears but only one mouth for good reason."

"Street Scene - Assisi" - 12 x 15 watercolor

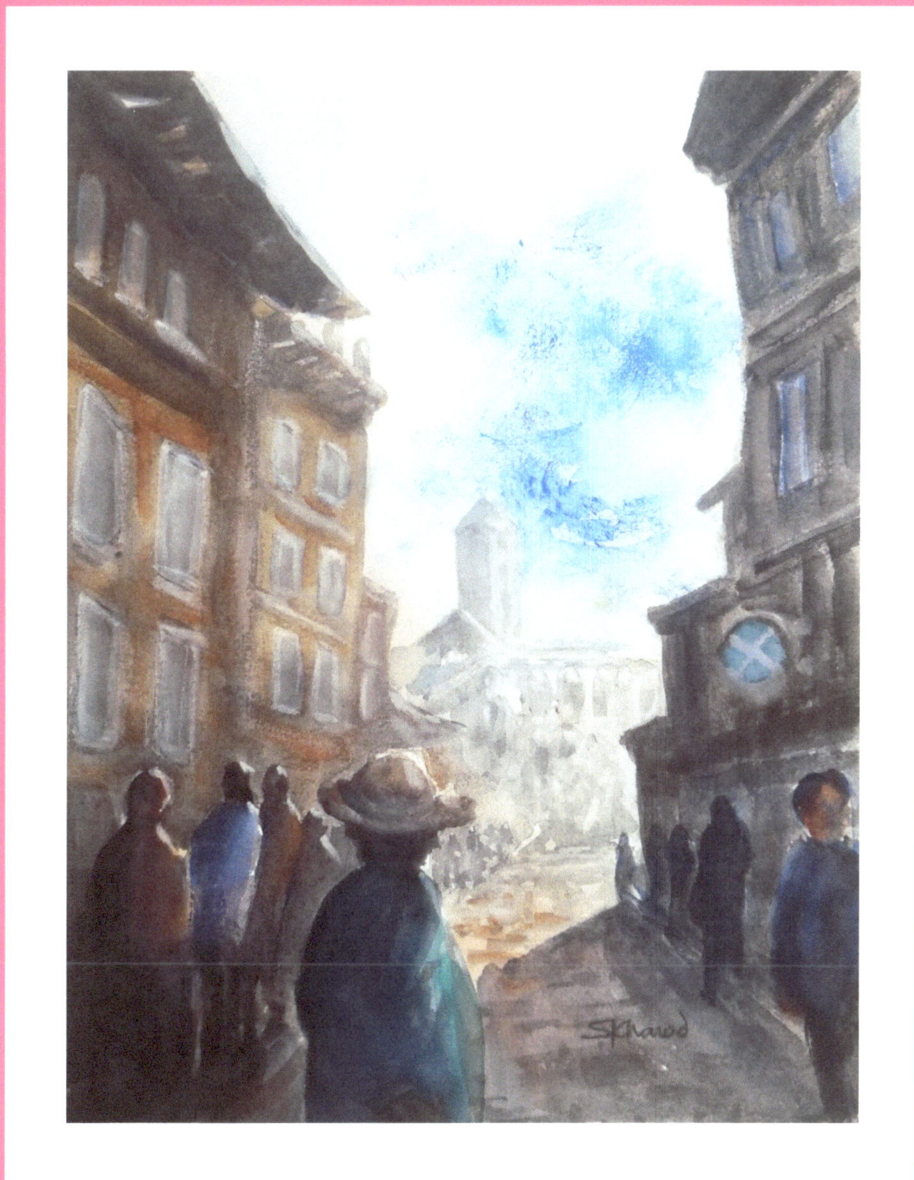

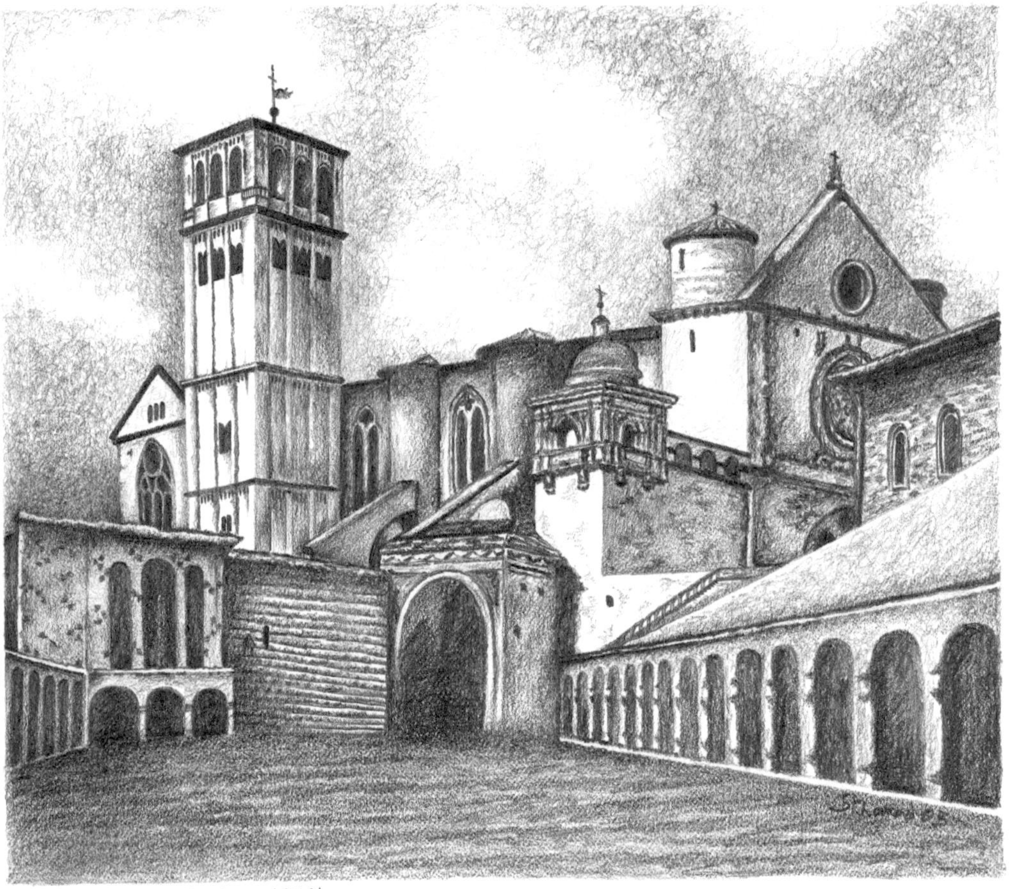

CHAPEL OF SAINT FRANCIS, ASSISI

A quiet moment to reflect

Nestled in the hills, a few hours from Rome in the heart of Umbria is Assisi. With its slower and gentler pace, it was a welcome change. It was less overrun by tourists than the bustling cities—it was a place for reflection.

Remnants of the powerful, stone wall that had once sheltered this fortress-city from invaders still stood solidly. Steep and narrow alleys intertwined within these walls and gave the city a unique charm. Though few people spoke English here, we found friendly faces all around.

The highlight of Assisi was the Basilica, a beautiful marble memorial built to honor St. Francis. Many devout pilgrims had come to circumambulate his tomb and offer their whispered prayers.

The hills of Assisi provided an earthy and tranquil backdrop for a memorial devoted to the saint who felt a unique kinship with nature.

"Chapel of Saint Francis" - 8 x 10 pencil, artist's collectior

Sometimes, I will repaint an entire painting, even if the original was good enough. Why do I bother painting another one if the initial effort was pretty good? And why do I usually prefer the second version? Because 'pretty good' and 'good enough' are not acceptable to me when it comes to my art.

After completing a painting, I put it on an easel and spend the next few days glancing at it from various vantage points, as I go about my daily tasks. I allow my subconscious mind to work on it. If something starts bothering me, I know it is my subconscious sending me a message, so I try to fix it. If I cannot fix it, I repaint. But, if I think my painting is 'pretty good' or 'good enough,' what I am truly saying is, "I know I didn't put in full effort, but am feeling lazy about doing so, so it is okay." (When actually, it is not.)

A caveat: even with full effort, I know my painting is not going to be at the level of a Turner, Sargent, or Monet (yet). This statement is based purely on self-knowledge. But I do know that the key to growth is to strive incessantly to improve without becoming arrogant, complacent, and definitely not lazy.

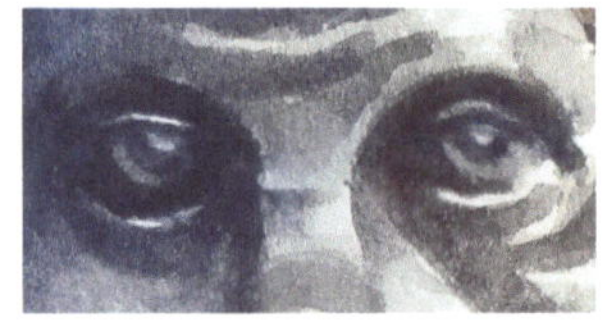

Don't settle for mediocrity. Strive to improve, yet remain humble.

Artists frequently receive critiques (both solicited and unsolicited) from people regarding their work. Ideally, critiques from third-parties should help an artist grow. But, too often, many artists feel judged, miserable, and failures because of what others say of their art.

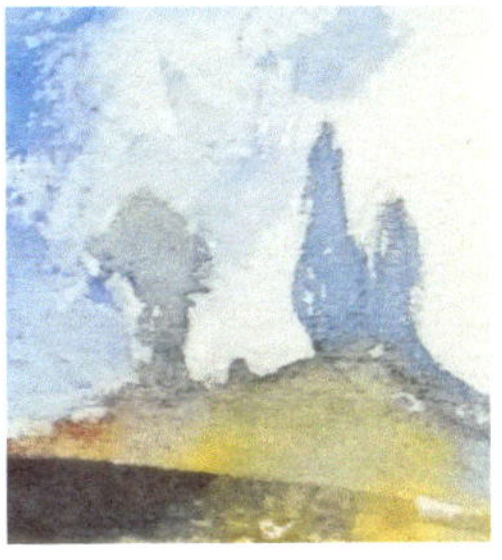

Don't judge yourself based solely on a critique of your last painting (or action).

My stint in advertising helped me understand and embrace negative critiques. As an art director, I would create hundreds of ideas for every assignment. I then self-critiqued those ideas and presented a handful to the creative director. Out of those, one, maybe two, would be selected by the creative director to show the client. My mentors taught me early on that when an idea is rejected by the creative director or the client, it is not a commentary on me as a person. It just means my ad concept was not right for that one situation.

In my post-advertising life, this ability to separate myself from my work (or from my actions) has helped when other people (whom I respect) critique my art or my actions because I accept their words as caring suggestions for my improvement. But I do not let those critiques determine how I feel about myself as a person.

FLORENCE AND PISA

"Visitors at Santa Maria del Fiore" - 11 x 15 watercolor

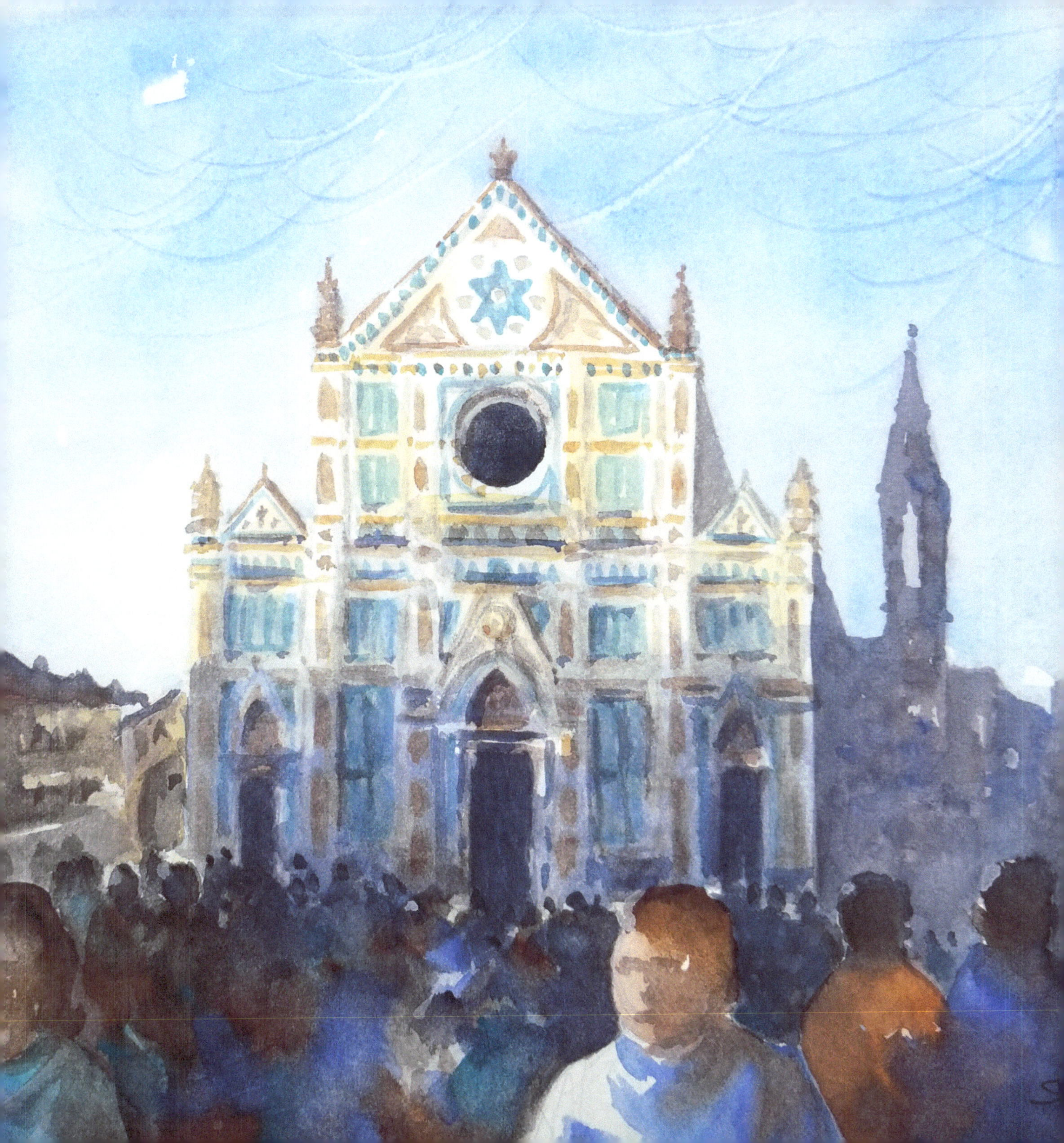

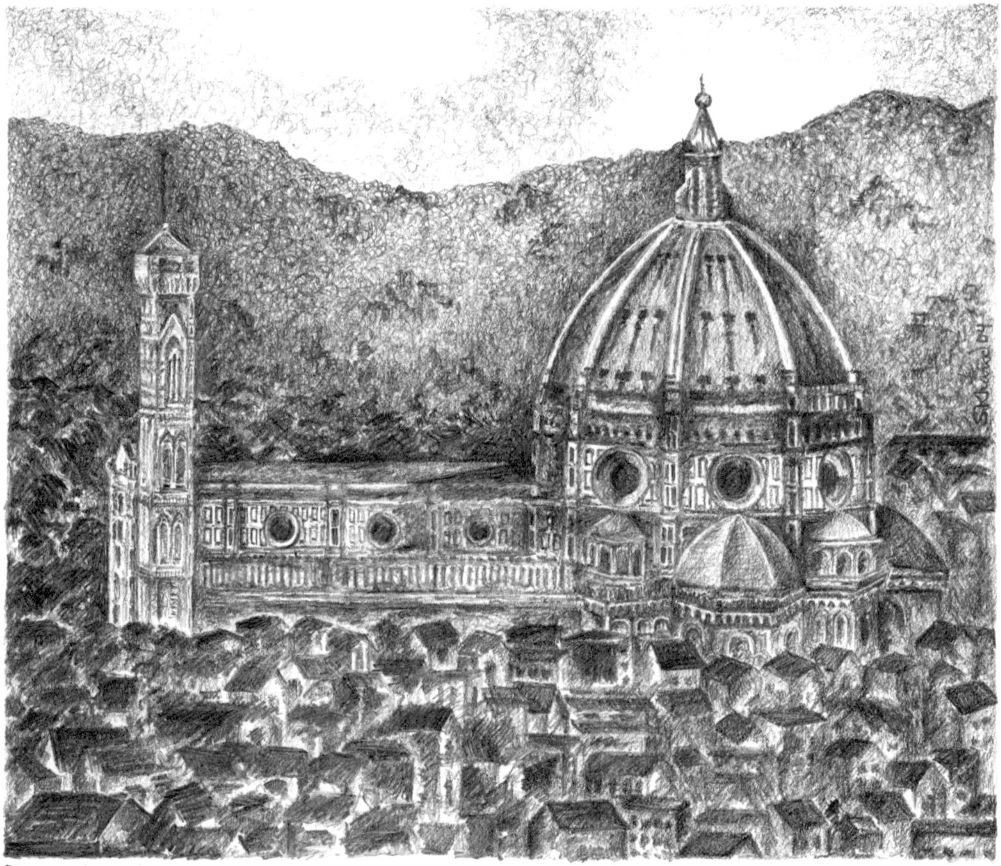

DUOMO, FLORENCE

"Do not attempt to climb the dome if you have a heart condition."

The first few steps were deceptively easy, causing us to scoff at the warning sign posted outside the Duomo. But all too soon, the stairs became steeper and began to spiral. As we circled around (distracting ourselves with the beautiful frescos on the dome's interior), we observed small, thin gaps, placed intermittently in the stone walls. They allowed a glimmer of hope and a gasp of fresh air in what had now become a dark, muggy, and breathless climb. The only way out was to keep going up and counting down the 463 excruciating steps to the top.

As we went further into the dome's interior, our ascent became steeper and tighter. The final dozen steps were literally an upward crawl and scramble to get to the pinnacle.

Ultimately, we emerged victorious onto the balcony where the views of Florence were breathtaking. And we did take many breaths of fresh air.

(The descent was much easier because we knew that open space, solid ground, and gelato were all waiting at the bottom.)

"Duomo" - 8 x 10 pencil, artist's collection

During our dark and uncomfortable climb, I would snatch every chance I had to peek out of the tiny windows of the Duomo. Each window provided a slightly different view of the city. Using every ounce of willpower in me to keep moving forward (and because there was really no option of turning back), I began to think about how life sometimes mimics this dome-climbing experience.

When obstacles arise (and they will), by pushing forward and moving with effort, determination, and perseverance, you will be able to surmount them. To help you face difficulties, the universe presents tiny windows, providing opportunities to experience happiness. If you look through them, you will see a view. Do you permit the view to give you happiness and sustenance, or not?

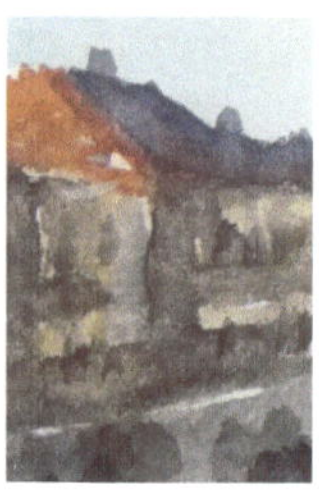

Your life's perspective is shaped by the windows you choose to look through and your response to the views you see.

"Campanile" - 8 x 10 pencil, artist's collection

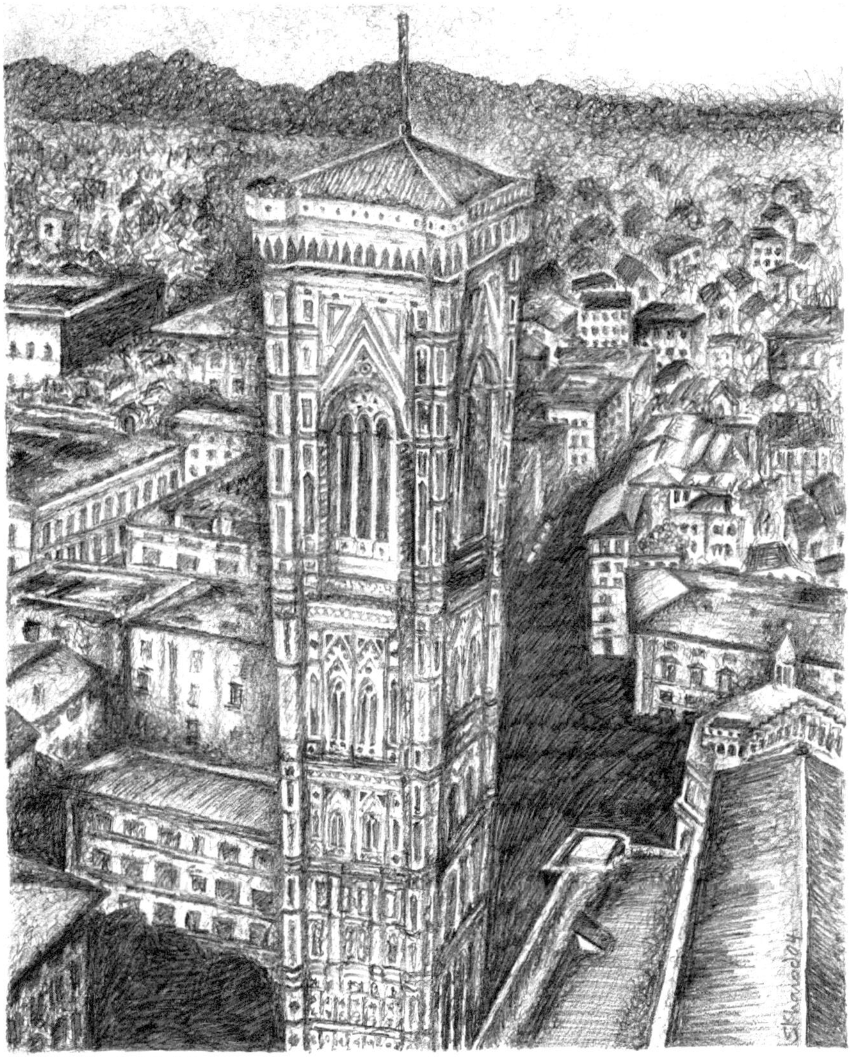

CAMPANILE, FLORENCE

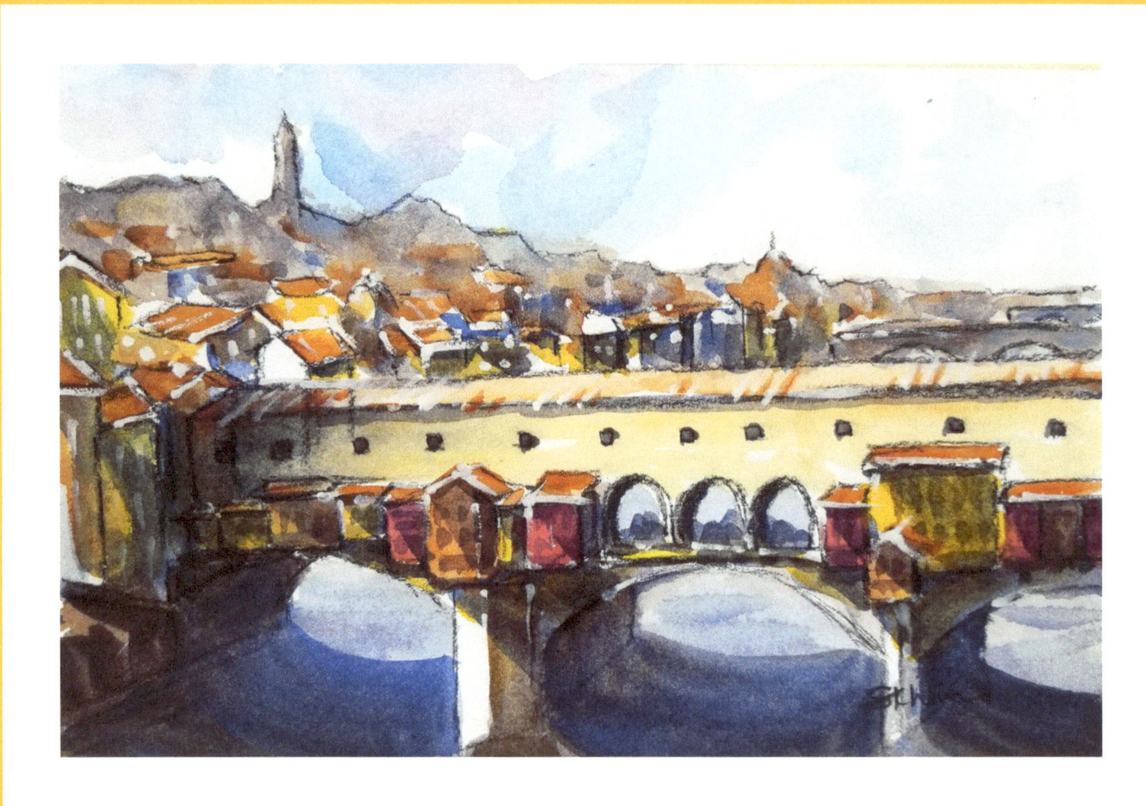

"I would like my pasta sunny-side up, please."

We looked at the menu. Eggplant Parmigiana, yes. Ravioli Pomodoro, sure. Fettuccini ai Funghi, good. Penne Arrabbiata, absolutely. And then we hit a speed bump—Spaghetti Americano. Wait, what?

Spaghetti Americano was spaghetti with marinara sauce, topped with a sunny-side-up egg and bacon. Americano? Really? Bacon and eggs make it Americano? I've since learned that some people actually enjoy their pasta in this way. But to us, calling it Americano was hilarious because no one we knew ate pasta this way in America.

Ketan and I are both vegetarian and teetotalers, so some may say we did not get the full foodie experience in Italy. That may be so, but we felt quite content with the amazing variety we did sample—case in point, real Italian pizza.

Even though Neapolitan pizza is considered the gold standard, Roman, Venetian, and Florentine pizza blew us away too. On our first day in Rome, we rolled out of the hotel and went in search of a local pizzeria. As we enjoyed slices topped with charred broccoli, grilled eggplant, buffalo mozzarella, and the most beautiful red sauce with a hint of balsamic vinegar, I decided I could be supremely content eating only pizza for the rest of our meals.

"Ponte Vecchio" - 7.5 x 11 watercolor

Honestly, what else do tourists go there to see?

Without even looking up, the bored attendant at Pisa's train station visitor's center flapped a map at us (route pre-drawn) and continued perusing her magazine. I believe she would have fallen from her stool had we asked for a different location.

Using our highlighted map, we made our way from the train station to the Leaning Tower in the Piazza dei Miracoli. According to anecdote, Galileo had conducted a free-fall experiment by dropping a cannonball and a musket ball off the top of the Leaning Tower to prove objects with unequal mass fell to the ground simultaneously. I wonder who volunteered to carry cannonballs up claustrophobic, winding, and leaning stairs for him?

We decided not to attempt this spiraling climb, but instead, remained on the ground. After taking the requisite photos (where we are 'holding the Tower up' with one finger and other things of that sort), we returned to Florence. And ate some gelato.

"Leaning Tower" - 8 x 10 pencil, artist's collection

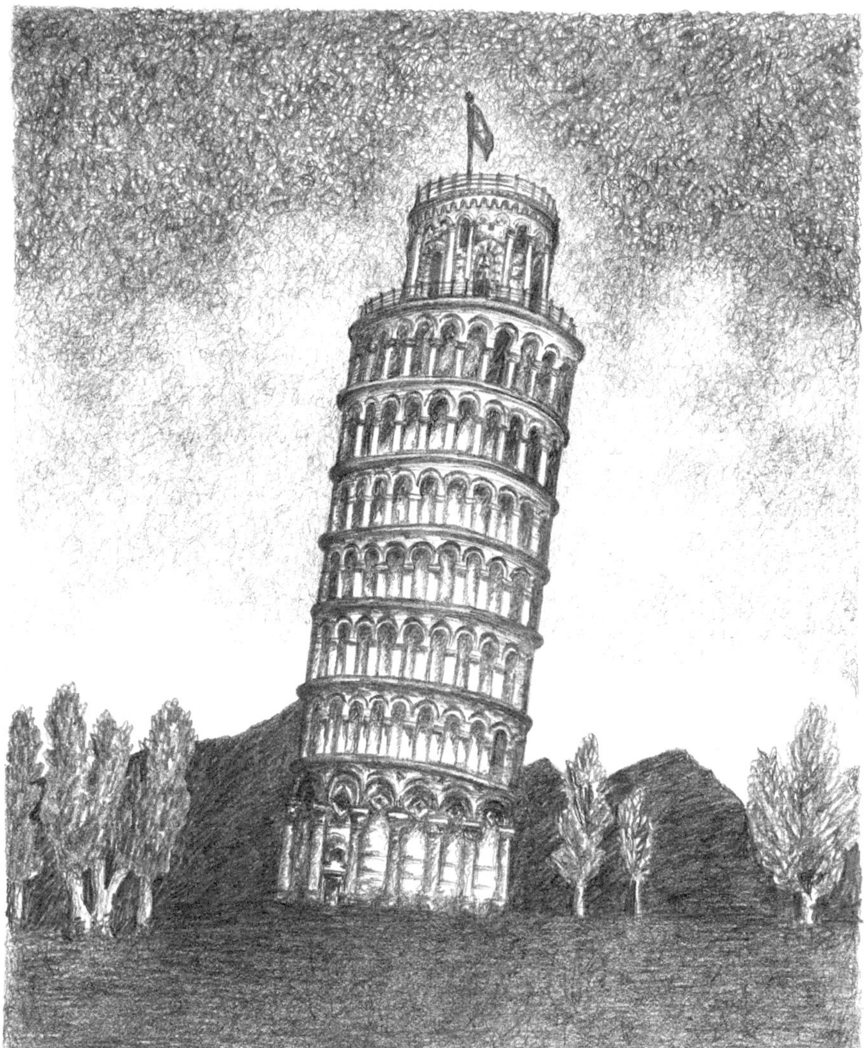

LEANING TOWER, PISA

I am often asked why I paint in watercolor. Common perception is that oils are the king of paints; acrylics are the exciting new kids on the block; and watercolors are children's paints or specifically for botanical illustrations.

This perception of watercolor is not fully accurate nor is it fair. True, watercolor doesn't require many specialized materials. Professional-quality pigments, brushes, and water will create all sorts of magic on paper. Most of us can remember using some sort of water-based paints and brushes as a child, with which we created refrigerator-worthy masterpieces. So, if it is so 'easy,' then why do even some professional artists feel watercolor is actually the most difficult medium of the three?

The first reason is that it is difficult to cover mistakes. Watercolor is transparent, not opaque like oil or acrylic. Imagine layering yellow and blue cellophane together. When light passes through the layers, it will look green. Watercolors work in the same way. The artist layers thin coats of diluted paint (called washes) on the paper. Light bounces off the paper, passes through the layered washes, and hits the eye. The science behind watercolors is what creates such colorful and glowing paintings.

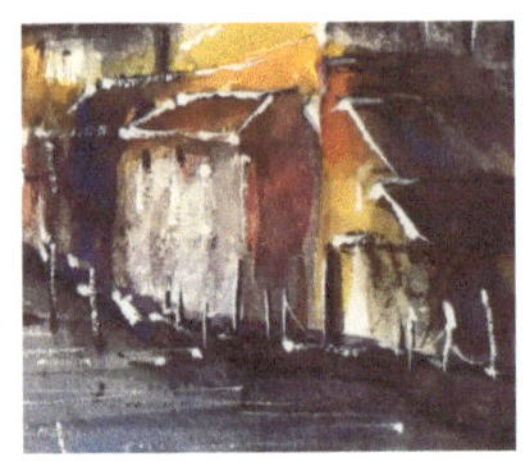

Some pigments can be 'lifted' off the paper using special techniques, but it is nearly impossible to lift a color completely and recapture the pure white of the original paper. Therefore, each brushstroke must be carefully planned beforehand as it will impact the finished piece.

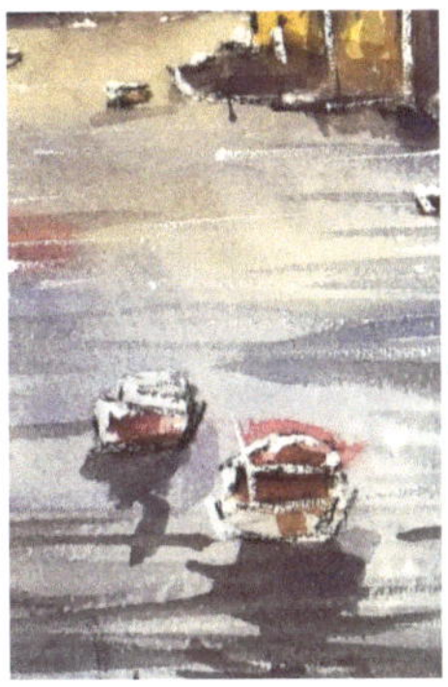

Another reason watercolor is difficult is that it can be very unpredictable. A painting is a carefully-orchestrated dance between the pigment-to-water ratio, the type of paper, and the artist's vision. A watercolor painter has to be willing to 'go with the flow'—literally—and discover how to harmonize the will of the wet paint with the will of the artist.

Think back to your childhood when you confidently held a paintbrush, painted bold strokes on paper, and then swished the brush in water, turning the water into a twilight-colored pool full of mystery.

As I hold a squirrel-hair brush in my hand, soak it in water, and touch it to the paint on my palette, I feel a creative adrenaline surge every time. And that is how I know watercolor is the right medium for me.

ROME AND THE VATICAN

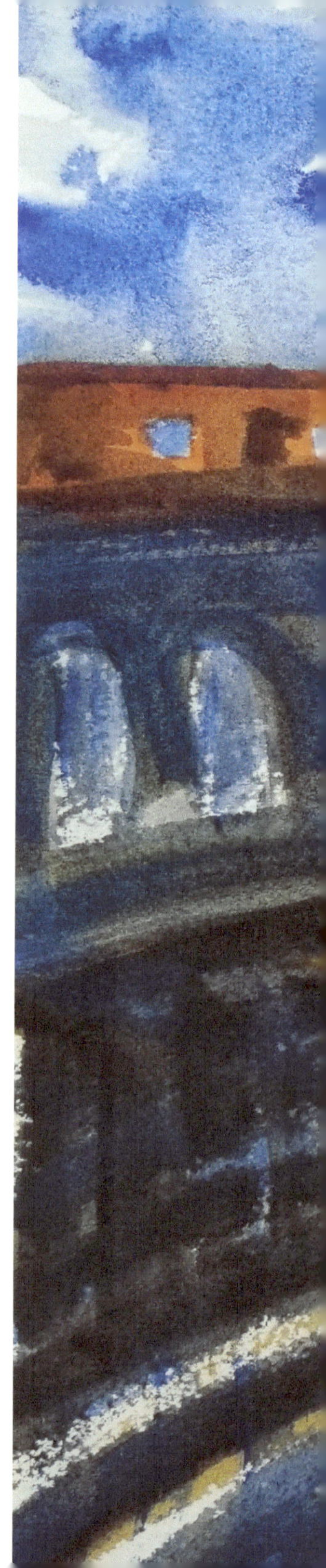

"Riot of Color at the Colosseum" - 12 x 15 watercolor

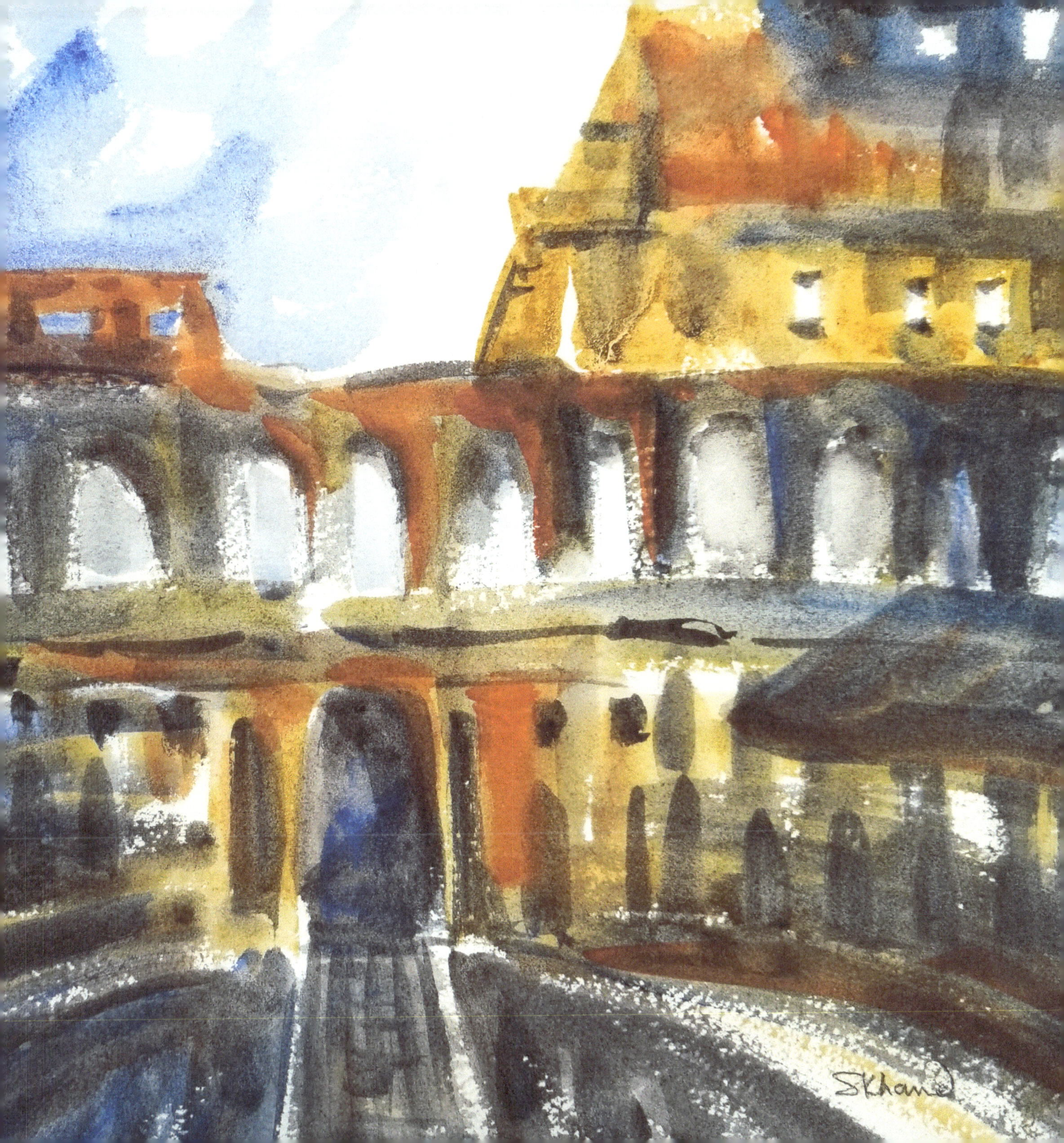
SKhan

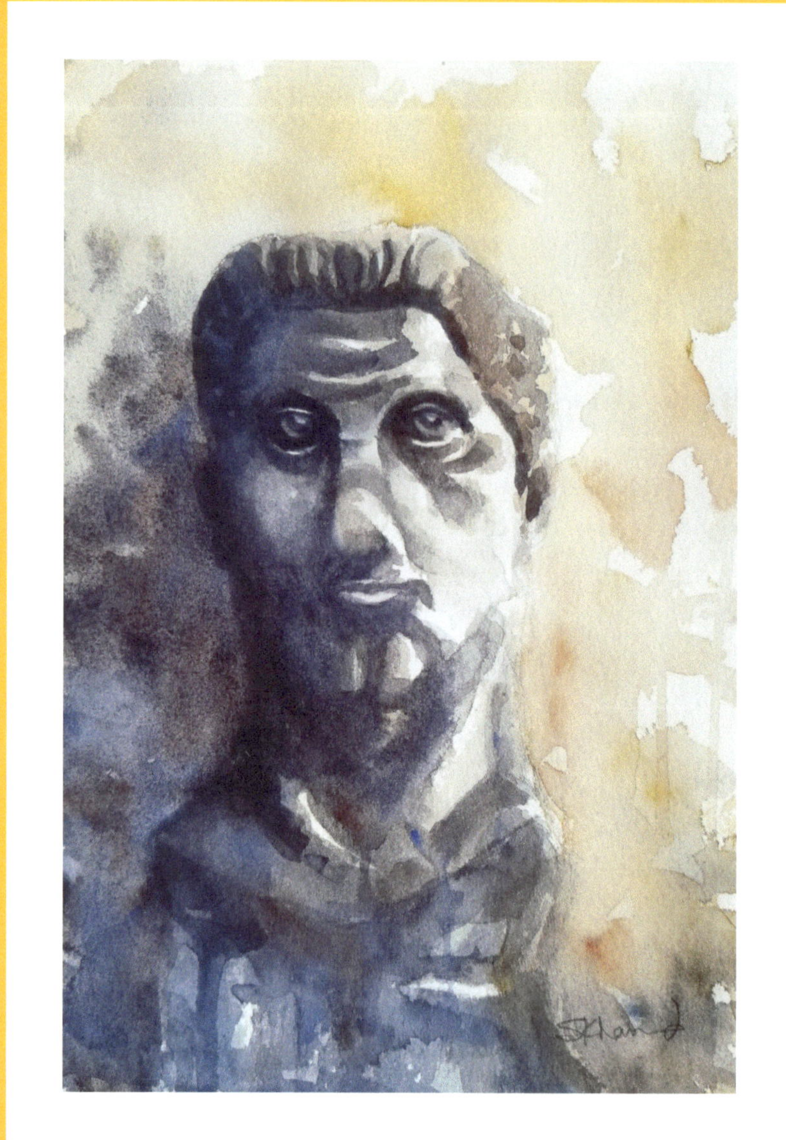

'Mr. Pronto'

The well-dressed gentleman, who managed the small flat we had booked for our last few days in Rome, was about to tell us its details when his phone rang. He answered the phone with an unexpected, "Pronto?" (rolling the 'r' quite dramatically). Ketan and I cast sidelong glances at each other and snickered silently, not knowing that this was how Italians actually answered the phone. After finishing his call, he turned his attention to us again.

Then, another call. "Prrronto?" Another glance and silent snicker. And, a few minutes later, yet another call. "Prrronto?"

Finally, we received the keys from 'Mr. Pronto' (as we promptly nicknamed him). Laughing our heads off while saying 'Prrronto?' to everything in sight, we were on our way, ready to experience modern Roman life by living like locals. Although, we had a few minor adventures—we didn't know how to turn on the stove and the washing machine flooded—'Mr. Pronto' was only a phone call away and always ready to help. "Prrronto?"

"Colossus of Capitolini" - 7 x 10 watercolor

The building in the bottom righthand corner

Tapping the bottom righthand corner of this drawing of the Spanish Steps, my former art history professor informed me, "Did you know Keats lived right here in this building—#26 Piazza di Spagna? And Goethe lived down the street?"

Many years ago, I had visited my former professor Dr. Alessandra Comini, armed with my sketchbook. As she flipped through it, she paused at this sketch. Her eyes lit up because she had noticed something highly interesting to her. I knew from experience what was coming next—fascinating tidbits and stories collected over a highly-distinguished career in art history and an adventurous life of globe-trotting.

To my surprise, the forthcoming stories were not about the Spanish Steps at all. Instead, she proceeded to tell me stories of the two writers John Keats and Johann Wolfgang von Goethe from their time spent in Rome. Although I can't recall the details of those stories now, I will never forget how animated and enthusiastic she became when she recognized and proceeded to narrate the history of the building in the bottom righthand corner.

"Spanish Steps" - 8 x 10 pencil, artist's collection

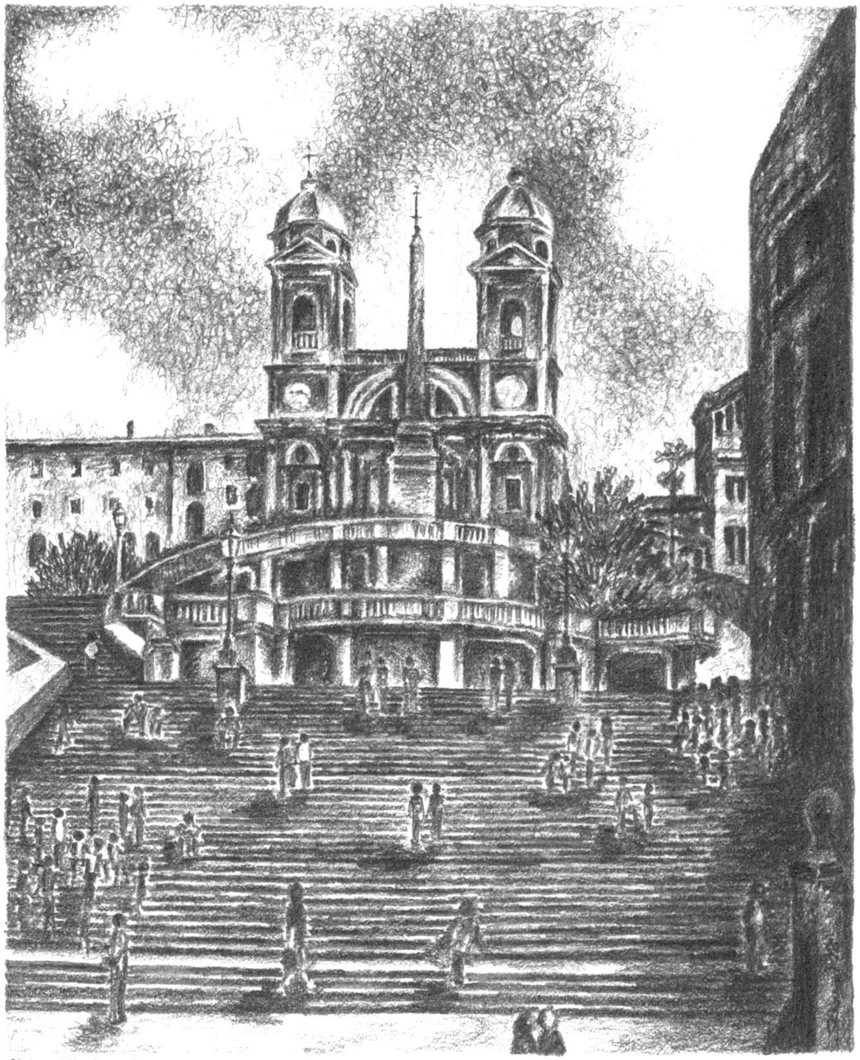

SPANISH STEPS, ROME

I did not like abstract art for a long time because it did not make sense to me. It appeared either childish, garish, or snobby. And I wondered, why so many of the world's prestigious museums, galleries, and art collectors placed such a high premium on it? After seeing Georgia O'Keeffe's abstract watercolors and Helen Frankenthaler's experiments in oils and acrylics, everything made sense.

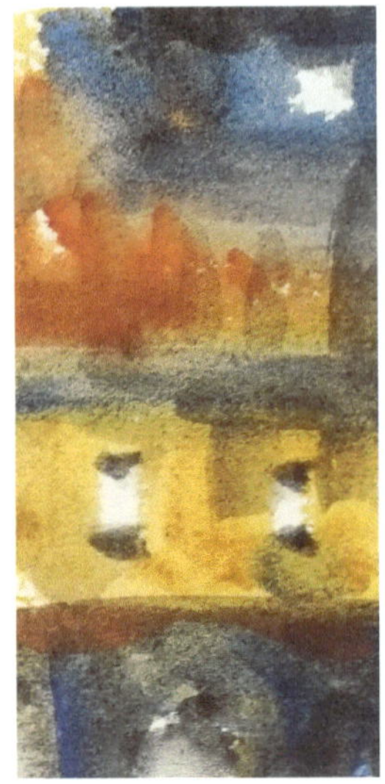

Abstract art is deceptively difficult to create. A work by an abstract master (for example, the 'drippery' of Jackson Pollock) belies the cranial activity and design knowledge involved in creating it. I have tried painting abstract watercolors and have created maybe three pieces (out of many attempts) that I truly liked.

Some people think abstract art looks like a child painted it. The reason is that both look spontaneous and bold, but the similarity ends there. An abstract created by a professional artist showcases a carefully-thought-out composition executed with a masterful touch.

Since the subject is never clearly defined, the painting pulls you, the viewer, in to interact with it and draw your own meaning and interpretation out of it. It does not become stale, nor is it easily forgotten.

The watercolors of O'Keeffe and the oils and acrylics of Frankenthaler helped me appreciate and open up to abstract art. O'Keeffe used minimal strokes, simple shapes, and bold colors to depict the natural world around her. Frankenthaler experimented with her technique to make oils and acrylics look translucent on canvas, resembling watercolor. What appeals to me, though, is the confidence that shines through both of their paintings.

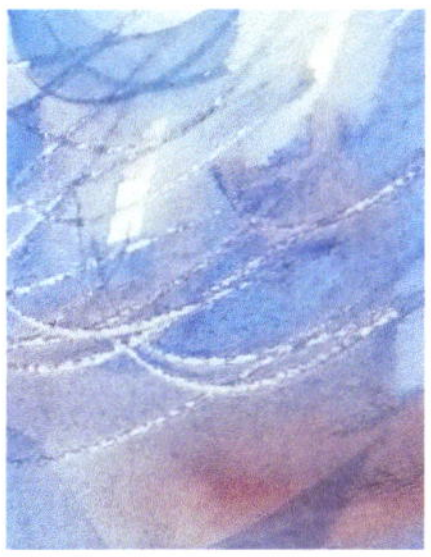

How does an artist learn to paint with confidence? Remember that bit about 'what went right?' The next part involves taking that 'right,' learning all about it, and doing it over and over until it becomes habit.

Self-reflection leads to self-understanding. Self-understanding leads to self-confidence.

As you start reflecting, you begin to understand yourself. You learn you have an inner voice and that voice is quite wise. As you learn to listen to your inner voice, you begin to feel self-confident, as if all answers can be found within you. That self-confidence is then reflected in your words and actions—and for the artist, in her paintings.

The oldest highway ... of the Western world

I was determined to see the Appian Way—the oldest highway ("... of the Western world," as Ketan kept adding). I was expecting to see a huge sign screaming, "Oldest highway!" or something like that. But, I forgot, we were in Europe, where they don't scream such things.

One morning, we took a local train south of the city. Then, we followed a map (maps of Rome are far superior to maps of Venice). Eventually, we came across a nondescript street with a small and equally nondescript street sign labeled, 'Via Appia Antica.' Laughing his head off, Ketan politely inquired, "Shall we go back now?"

After throwing him an evil glance, I agreed and we hoofed it back to the city. We reached Rome (after a seemingly endless walk) and refueled with the requisite gelatos (two, this time). We discovered we were near the Bocca della Verità (the Mouth of Truth). For me, as a fan of the film 'Roman Holiday,' this was a must-see attraction. My good-hearted husband humored me and we went to see it.

According to legend, if you told a lie and stuck your hand inside the statue's mouth, your hand would be bitten off. In typical Ketan style, he growled ferociously when I stuck my hand in the statue's mouth and made me jump. Then, he enjoyed his second belly laugh of the day at my expense.

"Bocca della Verità" - 7 x 10 watercolor

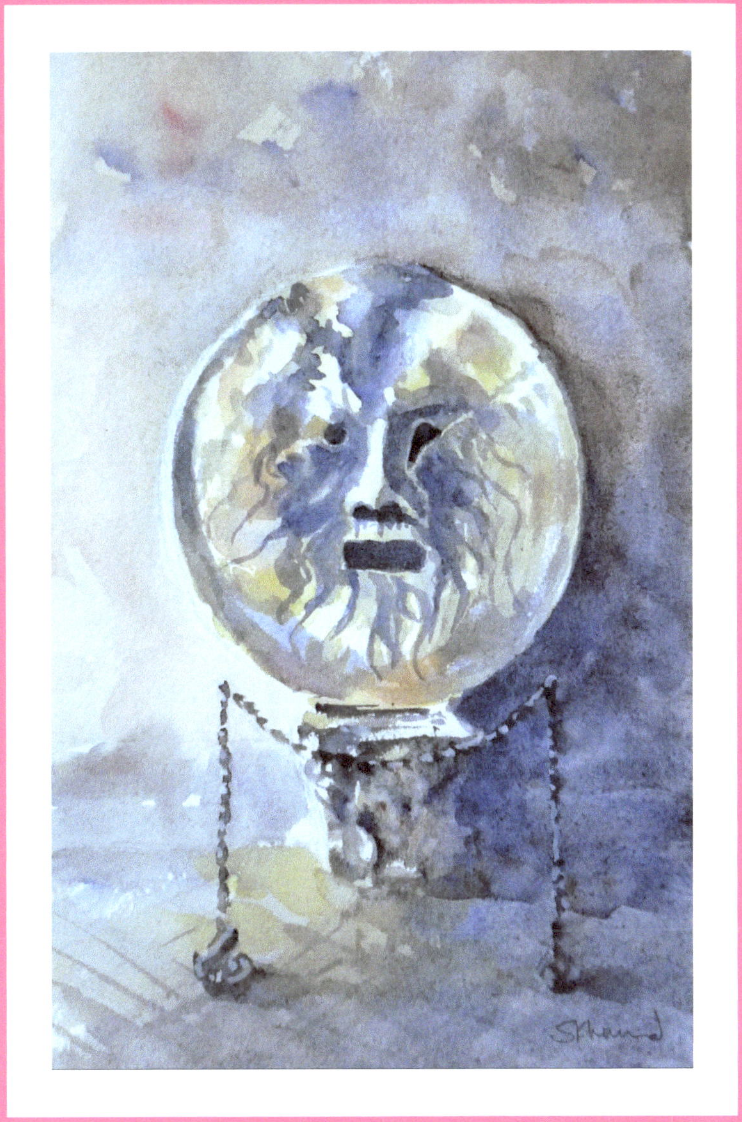

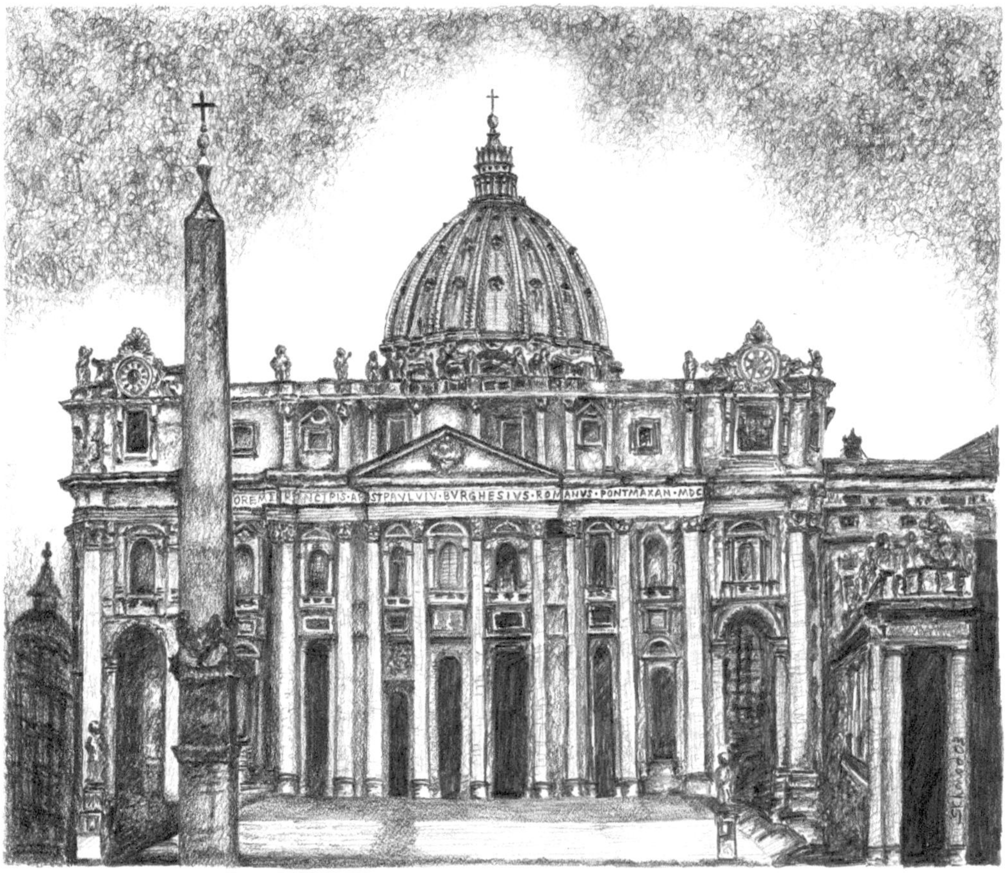

ST. PETER'S BASILICA, VATICAN CITY

“Our chapel is the longest in the world,” our tour guide claimed.

According to the marks on the floor, which compared the lengths of various notable chapels around the world, she was correct. The Sistine Chapel, in Vatican City near St. Peter’s Basilica, is 132 feet long and best known for its breathtaking ceiling painted by Michelangelo.

I stood underneath (mesmerized by the Biblical frescos as every other tourist is) and imagined lying on scaffolding a gazillion feet off the ground, painting intricate scenes.

My first concern—after being suspended so high—would be: what if paint drips into my eyes, mouth, and nose while I’m painting? My second concern would be: when I paint, I usually need to go close to my painting or step back to see different perspectives. So, would I have to keep going up and down scaffolding to accomplish this? Such trifles didn’t stop Michelangelo, fortunately.

For our Vatican tour, Ketan was better prepared and wore long pants. So, he wasn’t asked to go outside to purchase a pair of pants from the street vendors (who earned their livelihoods by selling pants outside the Vatican) like another unfortunate gentleman, who didn’t heed the tour books.

“St. Peter’s Basilica” - 8 x 10 pencil, artist’s collection

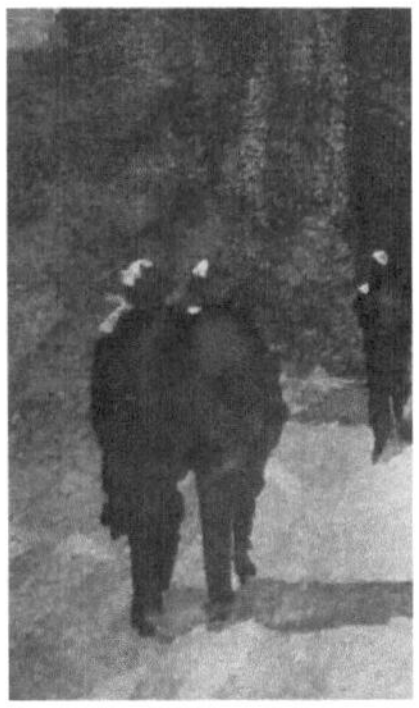

Creating art is a very satisfying adventure. Too often, I hear people say artists are born with special artistic talent, while the rest of humanity is not blessed in this way. Artists are born with artistic talent in the same way pilots, chefs, and firefighters are all born with their respective talents; it is a myth. Professional artists dedicate much time and effort towards learning and honing their artistic skills, same as how people in other professions develop their skills.

You, too, can create art and derive happiness from it—if you allow yourself to do so. Do not compare your art with anybody else's. Your journey as an artist is about *your* art experience; the same way your journey through Italy as a tourist would be about *your* travel experience.

If you have been to Italy, I hope my stories remind you of your own memories. If you have not visited Italy, I hope you will be able to go one day.

My sincere plea to you is to please make time to reflect upon your experiences, in the realms of your choosing. Life is a journey and, sometimes, even an adventure. And our reflections are our closest companions.

About the Author

Supriya Kharod lives in Austin with her husband Ketan and their three children. After initially working in advertising as an art director, she now prefers to have a paintbrush in hand, rather than a mouse. She is a primarily self-taught painter. In addition to watercolor and drawing, she enjoys vegetable gardening, practicing martial arts, playing tabla and guitar, spending time with family, and trying to perfect Neapolitan pizza at home.

Acknowledgments

Thank you for your advice and help with this fantastic journey: Casey Chapman-Ross, Sarojini Kanagala, Tiffany Harelick, Rasheeda Crayton, Alessandra Comini, Uma Parameswaran, and Raji Parameswaran. Sincere thanks to Sheila Snarr for teaching me how to draw and to Sonam Rehani and Mike and Vanderlyn Singley for believing in my artistic potential even before I believed in it myself. I am happy to have connected with so many people who have bought my art over the years. I hope you derive joy from it every day. And, most of all, my immense gratitude to my entire family—starting with the Source—and especially Ketan and the children for their love and support with everything always.

www.ingramcontent.com/pod-product-compliance
Ingram Content Group UK Ltd.
Pitfield, Milton Keynes, MK11 3LW, UK
UKHW061033310726
14089UKWH00010B/220
* 9 7 8 1 7 3 6 3 1 2 6 0 5 *